MY LITTLE
COCKTAIL BOOK

My Little Cocktail Book

200 Party Drinks

MURDOCH BOOKS

CONTENTS

NOTES FOR THE
—— LOUNGE LIZARD ——

COCKTAILS ARE SYNONYMOUS with glamourpusses, urban sophisticates and the cosmopolitan set, and with every single sip we cannot help but luxuriate in these glittering associations. From their rustic beginnings masking fiery bootleg liquor, cocktails are now on the cusp of a golden age, with spirit producers infusing classic spirits such as gin, vodka and tequila with exciting new flavours, promising infinite possibilities for those seeking the latest cocktail sensations.

There's no special mystique involved in cocktail making. It is an easy art to master and with a little dedicated practice you'll be serving drinks with flair and panache. All you need are a few simple implements, some basic ingredients, a steady hand, a highly developed sense of fun and a rampant imagination.

There's a cocktail in this book to suit any mood or occasion, from the snootiest soirée to splashing poolside frolics, smashing parties and after-dinner meltdowns. We'll even show you how to infuse spirits and whip up fruit purées for special 'signature' cocktails.

Before starting, a few quick words. Our recipes use a 20 ml (4 teaspoon) tablespoon, so if yours is a 15 ml (3 teaspoon) tablespoon, add an extra teaspoon per tablespoon. Recipes make one cocktail unless stated otherwise, using fresh, ripe fruit and fresh fruit juices unless otherwise specified. Finally, remember that although they may taste innocent, cocktails are highly intoxicating. So if you're hosting a cocktail party, offer plenty of food and non-alcoholic refreshments so your guests will remember what a fabulous time they had!

THE BAR
—————— ESSENTIALS ——————

YOU DON'T NEED TRUCKLOADS of fancy implements to create a classy cocktail, and most of them you'll find lurking somewhere in your kitchen.

One implement you'll definitely need to buy if you don't already have one is a cocktail shaker, available in two basic types. A standard shaker usually has three stainless steel pieces: a canister that holds the ice, a lid with an inbuilt strainer that seals tightly over the top, and a twist-off cap. The Boston shaker often has a mixing glass as its base, snugly overlapped by a stainless steel top. It doesn't have an inbuilt strainer, so you'll need a separate strainer to filter the drink during pouring. The most widely used is a hawthorn strainer, which has a distinctive circular head with a spring coil that fits sweetly around the metal half of a Boston shaker.

The other major implement most budding cocktail stars will need is an electric blender. If you're a total fanatic, invest in a heavy-duty model with a powerful motor and sturdy blades that can cope with whole ice cubes (check the manufacturer's instructions). If your blender is a little lightweight, you'll need to crush the ice cubes before putting them in the blender. To help your blades last longer, add the liquid ingredients to the blender first, then the ice.

Next, find yourself a large jug or pitcher with a pouring spout to use as a mixing glass; this is especially useful for making multiple quantities of mixed drinks. You'll also need measuring spoons and a jigger for measuring alcohol. Jiggers usually have double-sided cups, one holding 15 or 30 ml (½ or 1 oz), the other holding 45 or 60 ml (1½ or 2 oz).

A long-handled bar spoon (preferably stainless steel) is used for stirring cocktails and 'floating' ingredients in layered drinks. It can also be used for 'muddling' fruit and herbs, or you could buy a special muddler, which is essentially a wooden pestle, from specialist kitchen stores.

Ice, ice and more ice is essential to a cool cocktail, so you'll need plenty of ice-cube trays, an ice bucket for storing ice cubes, and a pair of tongs or an ice scoop for dispensing ice — never use your hands!

Other bits and bobs include a citrus squeezer, chopping board, sharp fruit knife, sharp vegetable peeler and zester. For those finishing touches, stock up on plain and coloured toothpicks, pretty cocktail umbrellas, swizzle sticks and straws of all description.

GLASS CLASS

PURISTS WILL INSIST ON USING the right glass for every drink. Short mixed drinks 'on the rocks' are served in an old-fashioned glass or tumbler; long mixed drinks are shaken, stirred or built in a highball glass or in a slightly deeper Collins glass. Cocktails without ice are poured into stemmed glasses to keep hot hands away from the drink. 'Short' drinks such as martinis are served in a triangular cocktail or martini glass. Champagne cocktails and some wine cocktails use a champagne flute, while cocktails containing egg yolks are usually dished out in goblets. Mixed or blended drinks are often served in a tulip-shaped glass. Other glasses include shot glasses, brandy balloons (enormous bowled glasses for swirling, sniffing and swilling fine brandies) and the sour glass, which resembles a champagne flute but has a shorter stem.

TRICKS OF THE TRADE

HERE'S A REALLY COOL TIP for making a really cool cocktail: have everything blisteringly cold. Chill all your ingredients before using, and chill the glasses too, or leave a scoop of ice in them while preparing your drinks. Always use fresh ice for each drink, and the best ingredients you

can source. Have all ingredients ready to go before you start mixing, shaking, stirring or building your drinks, and don't overfill shakers or mixers. To avoid spillage, never fill a glass to the brim, and remember to leave room for the garnish. When serving a cocktail, present the glass by its base or stem so you don't put hot, sticky handprints all over it. Finally, make each drink to order, as cocktails lose their 'verve' over time. Below are some techniques you'll find handy.

CRUSHING ICE Firmly wrap some ice cubes in a dry, clean tea towel and gently clobber them with a mallet or whack them against a solid bench. Bash up a big batch and stash it in the freezer.

BLENDING Purée the cocktail ingredients in a blender to a smooth, drinkable consistency, but don't overblend or you'll have a weak, watery concoction. Unless you have a heavy-duty blender, use crushed ice rather than ice cubes in your blender.

SHAKING Half-fill the cocktail shaker with crushed ice, add the other ingredients and vertically shake the canister vigorously until the shaker is frosty outside (10 seconds should do, but if your cocktail is very creamy or syrupy you might need to double the time). Strain into a chilled glass. Carbonated drinks should never be shaken or they'll lose their fizz.

STIRRING For sparkling clean looks, certain cocktails are stirred in a mixing glass or jug with a handful of ice cubes. This chills the alcohol quickly, without diluting it. The cocktail is then strained into a glass.

FLOATING Gently pour the liqueur or spirit into the glass over the back of a spoon. Add the ingredients in the order specified in the recipe and do not mix — the idea is to create a layered effect.

MUDDLING Grind, crush or mash fresh fruit or herbs with sugar (usually in a cocktail shaker), using a muddler or bar spoon to release all the flavours.

ADDING EGG WHITE Slide an egg white into a small glass receptacle and use a sharp knife to 'cut' or slice away a portion of egg white to slip into your drink.

SNAZZY ICE CUBES Freeze fruit juice in an ice-cube tray, perhaps with some mint leaves or diced fruit.

SOME CLASSIC
—————— TWISTS ——————

MANY RECIPES IN THIS BOOK will mention the garnish traditionally used to grace a particular drink. Citrus twists and citrus spirals receive special mention here as they are a favourite little flourish, but with the more outlandish tropical concoctions let your imagination run riot — use as many skewered fruits, swizzle sticks and tiny parasols as you fancy!

CITRUS TWIST Use a citrus peeler or very sharp knife to slice a thin, wide strip of peel from the citrus fruit, avoiding the bitter white pith. Make a small cut across the peel and twist it in opposite directions (do this over the drink to release a fine spray of zesty oils) and serve the twist on the side of the glass or in the drink.

_CITRUS SPIRAL Use a citrus peeler, zester or sharp knife to slice a long, continuous strip of peel from the fruit. The longer the peel, the greater the curl.

FOR A SPECIAL
—————— TOUCH ——————

MANY RECIPES CALL FOR SUGAR SYRUP, which you can buy or very easily make. Simply place equal quantities of water and sugar in a saucepan and stir well to dissolve the sugar. Bring to the boil, reduce the heat and simmer until reduced by half. Allow to cool, pour into an airtight container and refrigerate.

FRUIT PURÉES give fruity cocktails that extra lift. All you do is blend fresh fruit with a fruit liqueur, pour it into a 500 ml (17 oz/2 cups) airtight container, seal and refrigerate. Try these! Mango Blend the flesh of 4 ripe mangoes with 60 ml (2 oz) mango liqueur. Peach Blend 6–8 sliced peaches with 60 ml (2 oz) peach liqueur. Raspberry Blend two punnets of raspberries with 60 ml (2 oz) raspberry liqueur.

Strawberry Blend 500 g (1 lb 2 oz) of hulled strawberries with 60 ml (2 oz) strawberry liqueur.

INFUSED SPIRITS have taken off in a big way. Vodka alone is now available in fantastic flavours such as bison grass, vanilla, honey, citrus, peach, blackcurrant, sloe berry, pepper and chocolate. But why not be your own mixmaster and infuse your own potions? Vodka is the perfect starting base as it is neutral in colour and flavour. Use good-quality vodka, start with small batches and plan ahead: you'll need to steep it for at least three days. The quantities here will infuse a 1 litre (35 oz) bottle of vodka, gin, vermouth or tequila, so adjust the ingredients accordingly. Basil or mint 8–10 basil or mint leaves, wrapped in a thin muslin cloth. Blueberry 15 blueberries. Cinnamon 2 cinnamon sticks. Chilli 5 red bird's eye chillies. Coffee 10–15 whole roasted coffee beans. Lemon grass 1–2 stems. Lychee 8–10 peeled, seeded lychees — if tinned, add 30 ml (1 oz) lychee syrup. Peach 3 sliced peaches. Raspberry 15 raspberries. Strawberry 6 sliced strawberries. Vanilla 2 vanilla beans, sliced down the middle. Watermelon 10 nice chunks.

HOW TO DO IT Pour your chosen spirit into a 1 litre (35 oz) airtight or screwcap container (reserve the empty bottle). Add the other ingredients, seal the lid tightly and store in a dark, cool, dry place for 3–5 days. Gently shake the mixture now and then and check how the flavour is developing. The longer you leave it, the stronger it will become. If it becomes too strong, dilute it with unflavoured spirits until it reaches your preferred intensity. When you're done, strain the liquid into the original bottle and store in the freezer, ready to drink.

BUBBLES

Nothing speaks of celebration,
exhilaration, excitation and exaltation
quite as eloquently as the popping of a
Champagne cork and the gentle tinkle of
clinking flutes. Champagne cocktails, fizzes,
sparkles and spritzers: all that whispers of
laughter and joy is here in abundance to
mark life's most precious moments.
So bring out some icy cold bottles of your
best bubbly stuff and get ready to shine!

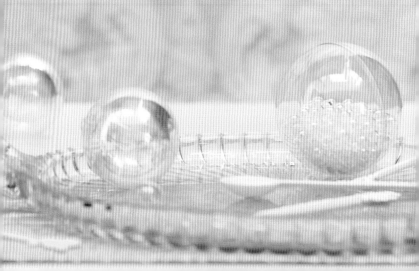

ELEGANCE
AND PANACHE

LIFE ISN'T ALL BEER AND SKITTLES — some occasions call for a dash of elegance and panache. And what could be more civilized and refined than sipping a Champagne cocktail while dressed to the nines and practising the gentle art of conversation in congenial company? The cocktails in this chapter are for special times — births, marriages, anniversaries — or whenever life's been a little flat and you need a fast injection of fun or exuberant decadence. But first to a point of protocol. Champagne refers to the celebrated liquid produced in the French region of the same name, whose branding is zealously protected. Other bubblies made using the same technique are known by the more prosaic moniker of sparkling wine, but the end result is arguably equally delightful. Whether you imbibe Champagne or sparkling wine, these ambrosial cocktails deserve the best you can afford. And make sure you give your bubblies a really good chilling to bring out their luscious bouquet and mouthfeel. The cocktails in this chapter call on heavenly additions such as brandy, amaretto and Grand Marnier; a cornucopia of liqueurs — peach, ginger, vanilla, blackcurrant, blackberry and strawberry, as well as limoncello and blue curaçao — and classic spirits such as Campari, gin and vodka. Other bar basics include soda water, sugar syrup, Angostura bitters and the odd bottle of pinot noir. So now that we've covered the essentials, let's get popping!

CLASSIC
— CHAMPAGNE —
COCKTAIL

Fashions come and fashions go but the
true classic is untouchable.

1 sugar cube
dash of Angostura bitters
30 ml (1 oz) brandy
chilled Champagne or sparkling wine

Place the sugar cube in a chilled champagne flute.
Add the bitters, then the brandy. Slowly top up with
Champagne or sparkling wine.

CHAMPAGNE
— BERRY —
COCKTAILS

Serve these exquisite berry-laden bubbles on a
silver platter in your finest flutes and wait for
the accolades to roll in.

6 sugar cubes
dash of Angostura bitters
zest of 1 lime, very finely sliced
200 g (7 oz) blackberries, raspberries,
blueberries or strawberries
1 bottle of chilled Champagne or sparkling wine

Place a cube of sugar in six chilled champagne flutes and
add a dash of bitters to each. Divide the lime zest and
berries among the flutes and slowly top up with
Champagne or sparkling wine.

SERVES 6.

POIRE
ROYALE

When life goes a little pear-shaped, this sublime
nectar will make you feel like a princess again.

15 ml (1/2 oz) Poire William
15 ml (1/2 oz) peach liqueur
1 teaspoon elderflower cordial
chilled Champagne or sparkling wine
thin pear slice

Pour the Poire William, peach liqueur and elderflower
cordial into a chilled champagne flute, then slowly
top up with Champagne or sparkling wine.
Garnish with a pear slice.

BARTENDER'S TIP
You can buy elderflower cordial, or make it at home.
Boil 2 litres (70 oz/8 cups) water with 1 kg (2 lb 4 oz)
sugar until the sugar dissolves and the syrup thickens
slightly. Pour it onto six elderflower heads in a sterile glass
jar and steep overnight. Strain, add lemon juice to taste
and keep refrigerated for a few days. Dilute with
water, if necessary.

APPLE AND
CALVADOS
CHAMPAGNE
COCKTAIL

Apples were nothing but trouble for Eve,
but a couple of these might just be your ticket
to the garden of Eden.

15 ml (1/2 oz) Calvados
15 ml (1/2 oz) clear apple juice
chilled Champagne or sparkling wine

Pour the Calvados and apple juice into a chilled
champagne flute, then carefully top up with
Champagne or sparkling wine.

BARTENDER'S TIP
This is one of those rare occasions when fresh isn't best.
Freshly squeezed apple juice makes for a cloudy cocktail,
so to keep it sparkling, use the bottled variety.

LIMONCELLO
COCKTAIL

From sun-drenched lemon groves along the sparkling coast of Naples comes lovely limoncello to make this cocktail shine.

10 ml (1/4 oz) lime juice
15 ml (1/2 oz) limoncello
chilled Champagne or sparkling wine

Pour the lime juice and limoncello into a chilled champagne flute, then slowly top up with Champagne or sparkling wine.

SAVOY

As opulent and lavish as the celebrated hotel
that shares its name, this drink is all style.

15 ml (1/2 oz) Campari
15 ml (1/2 oz) ruby red grapefruit juice
15 ml (1/2 oz) lychee juice
chilled Champagne or sparkling wine
orange twist

Pour the Campari, grapefruit juice and lychee juice
into a chilled champagne flute, then slowly top up
with Champagne or sparkling wine. Garnish with
a twist of orange.

— GIN PALACE —

A palace made of gin? Too many of these and you'll
be seeing castles in the air and clouds in your coffee.

15 ml (1/2 oz) gin
15 ml (1/2 oz) blackberry liqueur
10 ml (1/4 oz) vanilla liqueur
chilled Champagne or sparkling wine
3 blueberries

Pour the gin, blackberry liqueur and vanilla liqueur into a
chilled champagne flute. Slowly top up with Champagne or
sparkling wine and garnish with blueberries.

GIN FIZZ

Make your night a fizz not a fizzle
with long, cool, sparkly gin.

ice cubes
15 ml (1/2 oz) gin
15 ml (1/2 oz) lemon juice
10 ml (1/4 oz) sugar syrup
soda water
lemon wedge

Half-fill a cocktail shaker with ice. Add the gin, lemon juice
and sugar syrup, then shake well. Strain into a highball
glass half-filled with ice, then top up with soda water.
Garnish with a small wedge of lemon.

FLIRTINI

Pining for a flirty encounter? Find a sexy stranger, flutter those lashes and sigh languorously as you nibble that cherry.

15 ml (1/2 oz) pineapple vodka
15 ml (1/2 oz) pineapple juice
chilled Champagne or sparkling wine
maraschino cherry

Pour the vodka and pineapple juice into a chilled martini glass. Slowly top up with Champagne or sparkling wine and garnish with a maraschino cherry.

BARTENDER'S TIP
Many vodka companies are now producing pineapple vodka, but if you can't find it you can use plain vodka.

BELLINI

Born in 1948 in Harry's Bar and named after an Italian painter, the bellini tells the secrets of Venice in the summer.

15 ml (1/2 oz) peach liqueur
30 ml (1 oz) peach juice or nectar
chilled Champagne or sparkling wine

Pour the peach liqueur and peach juice into a chilled champagne flute. Slowly top up with Champagne or sparkling wine.

SCARLET
BELLINI

If the original version isn't sinful enough,
try this decadent crimson concoction.

15 ml (1/2 oz) peach liqueur
30 ml (1 oz) blood orange juice
chilled Champagne or sparkling wine
half a blood orange slice

Pour the peach liqueur and orange juice into a chilled
champagne flute. Slowly top up with Champagne or
sparkling wine. Garnish with half a slice of blood orange.

PINOT SANGRIA SPRITZERS

A fruitful way to take your glass of daily red
— just what the good doctor ordered.

ice cubes
1 bottle of pinot noir
250 ml (9 oz/1 cup) orange juice
1 orange, sliced into half moons
1 lemon, sliced into half moons
1 lime, sliced into half moons
500 ml (17 oz/2 cups) chilled lemon or lime soda water

Put the ice cubes, pinot noir and orange juice in a large jug
and stir well. Add the sliced fruit and leave in the fridge to
chill for 30 minutes. Add the soda water and serve in tall
glasses, with extra ice if you like.

SERVES 4–6.

CRANBERRY
— AND VODKA —
SPARKLE

Adds colour to your cheeks and a little
sparkle to your step.

ice cubes
125 ml (4 oz/1/2 cup) cranberry juice
125 ml (4 oz/1/2 cup) lemonade or mineral water
10 ml (1/4 oz) lime juice
15 ml (1/2 oz) vodka

Half-fill a mixing jug with ice. Pour in the cranberry
juice, lemonade or mineral water, lime juice and vodka.
Stir, then pour into a highball glass.

BLUEBERRY
SOUR

Pucker up for a perky experience that
kisses you right back.

1 tablespoon frozen lemon sorbet
15 ml ($1/2$ oz) vodka
chilled Champagne or sparkling wine
6 blueberries

Spoon the sorbet into a chilled martini glass. Pour in
the vodka and slowly top up with Champagne or
sparkling wine. Garnish with blueberries.

CHIC

If you feel sweetness is a plague and your wit and palate veer sharply towards the dry side, you might find these elegant cocktails too sexy for words. Oozing style and sophistication, these are drinks for classy, confident types capable of taking the bitter with the sweet. Acerbic, astringent and invigorating aperitifs mix it with many a dry, wry, macerating martini to sharpen the mind as well as the appetite.

BITTERSWEET
SEDUCTION

GIN, VODKA AND VERMOUTH are the classic culprits behind this searingly smart set of seductive favourites and memorable martinis. Here our vodka takes on some ultra-cool associations, infused with mandarin, bison grass and sloe berry. Campari makes a strong impression too, with a special guest appearance by its somewhat less bitter Italian cousin, aperol. You'll find the odd liqueur from the more exotic end of the flavour spectrum: sweet and sour apple schnapps, lychee liqueur, vanilla liqueur and the oh-so-Continental limoncello. Japanese sake makes a surprise debut, emphasizing the cosmopolitan connections of this highly select company. A major bittersweet contributor to these bracing libations is a full-throttled squeeze of fresh citrus juice, from lemon and lime to blood orange and ruby grapefruit, with cranberry juice offering an equally tart rejoinder. Of course you'll need buckets of ice as these cocktails must be served arctically cold. And in keeping with our disapproval of ostentatious frippery, we shall also keep our garnishes simple and classy: olives, a twist of lemon or orange, a wedge of lime, the odd maraschino cherry and a pearl onion or two. Stock up on soda water, check your sugar syrup levels and maybe even invest in some lime juice cordial, by which we mean the syrupy, thick cordial extracted from real limes — definitely not the impossibly green cordial found on supermarket shelves!
Over to you ...

— DRY MARTINI —

Proffer a tray of these and there won't
be a dry eye in the house.

ice cubes
1 teaspoon dry vermouth
90 ml (3 oz) gin
green olive or a lemon twist

Half-fill a mixing glass with ice. Add the dry vermouth,
stir to coat the ice, then strain out the excess. Add the
gin, then stir and strain into a chilled martini glass.
Garnish with a green olive or a twist of lemon.

—— VODKATINI ——

If gin brings a tear to the eye, try the
martini's milder cousin.

ice cubes
10 ml (1/4 oz) dry vermouth
80 ml (2 1/2 oz) vodka
lemon twist

Half-fill a mixing glass with ice. Add the dry vermouth,
stir to coat the ice, then strain out the excess. Add the
vodka, then stir and strain into a chilled martini glass.
Garnish with a twist of lemon

PERFECT
— MARTINI —

The perfect version of the perfect drink promises
the perfect start to a perfect evening.

ice cubes
60 ml (2 oz) gin
15 ml (1/2 oz) dry vermouth
15 ml (1/2 oz) sweet vermouth
green olives or a lemon twist

Half-fill a mixing glass with ice. Pour in the gin, dry
vermouth and sweet vermouth and stir. Strain into
a chilled martini glass and garnish with green olives
or a twist of lemon.

SAKETINI

The martini takes a Japanese twist
with a bracing shot of sake.

ice cubes
15 ml (1/2 oz) sake
75 ml (2 1/2 oz) vodka
dash of dry vermouth
thin cucumber baton

Half-fill a mixing glass with ice. Add the sake, vodka and
a dash of dry vermouth. Stir, then strain into a chilled
martini glass and garnish with a thin baton of cucumber.

— GIN FRENCH —

Pale and herbal, dry vermouth is also called French
vermouth. This French kiss is not for the
faint of heart.

ice cubes
70 ml (2¼ oz) gin
20 ml (½ oz) dry vermouth
lemon twist

Half-fill a mixing glass with ice. Add the gin and
vermouth, then strain into a chilled cocktail glass.
Garnish with a twist of lemon.

SOUR APPLE
—— MARTINI ——

When the martini mysteriously fell out of favour,
a little apple schnapps brought it back into flavour.

ice cubes
45 ml (1^1/$_2$ oz) sweet and sour apple schnapps
45 ml (1^1/$_2$ oz) vodka
10 ml (1/4 oz) lime juice
thin apple slice
lime spirals

Half-fill a cocktail shaker with ice. Add the schnapps,
vodka and lime juice. Shake vigorously and strain
into a chilled martini glass. Garnish with a floating
apple slice and spirals of lime.

— GIN AND IT —

Say *buon giorno* to this Italian classic. It's sweet, red and spicy and it'll knock your socks off.

70 ml (2¼ oz) gin
20 ml (½ oz) sweet red vermouth
maraschino cherry

Pour the gin and vermouth unchilled into a cocktail glass.
Garnish with a maraschino cherry.

GIBSON

Once the drink of free-thinking, high-spirited girls about town, it's high time to put the gibson's name back up in lights.

ice cubes
80 ml (2½ oz) gin
10 ml (¼ oz) dry vermouth
pearl onion

Half-fill a mixing glass with ice. Add the gin and vermouth, then stir. Strain into a chilled cocktail glass and garnish with a pearl onion.

CAMPARI CRUSH

Schoolgirl crushes are a thing of the past when the
grown-up version tastes so much sweeter.

crushed ice
30 ml (1 oz) gin
30 ml (1 oz) Campari
ruby red grapefruit juice
lime wedge

Fill a highball glass with crushed ice. Add the gin
and Campari, then top up with grapefruit juice. Squeeze
a lime wedge into the glass and add the squeezed
wedge to the drink.

—KNICKERBOCKER—

This celebrated cocktail takes its name from the
New York hotel where the first martini was
reputedly mixed.

ice cubes
15 ml (1/2 oz) dry vermouth
15 ml (1/2 oz) sweet vermouth
60 ml (2 oz) gin
slice of lemon

Half-fill a mixing glass with ice. Add the dry vermouth,
sweet vermouth and gin. Strain into a chilled martini glass,
squeeze a slice of lemon over the glass and add the
squeezed lemon to the cocktail.

KABUKI

As stylized as its namesake, this drink puts on an impressive show. So will you after one too many.

lemon wedge
salt
60 ml (2 oz) sake
15 ml (1/2 oz) lime juice cordial
15 ml (1/2 oz) sugar syrup
15 ml (1/2 oz) lime juice
15 ml (1/2 oz) Cointreau
6 ice cubes
lime twist

Wipe the lemon wedge around the rim of a martini glass, then dip the rim in salt to coat. Chill the glass. Place the sake, lime juice cordial, sugar syrup, lime juice, Cointreau and ice in a heavy-duty blender. Blend well and pour into the prepared glass. Garnish with a twist of lime.

CITRUS
BLUSH

Enough to make a maiden blush, this zesty cocktail
is specially formulated to drown your sorrows.

crushed ice
15 ml (1/2 oz) lime juice
15 ml (1/2 oz) limoncello
45 ml (11/2 oz) gin
ruby red grapefruit juice
lime twist

Half-fill a tall glass with crushed ice. Add the lime
juice, limoncello and gin. Stir well to combine,
top up with ruby red grapefruit juice and garnish
with a twist of lime.

—LIFE'S GOOD—

Amble through this cocktail as you would a rambling
orchard on a clear, sunny day.

ice cubes
45 ml (1½ oz) sloe berry vodka
15 ml (½ oz) lychee juice
15 ml (½ oz) cranberry juice
15 ml (½ oz) strawberry purée (see recipe on page 17)
lime wedge

Half-fill a cocktail shaker with ice. Add the vodka, lychee
juice, cranberry juice and strawberry purée. Shake
vigorously and strain into a chilled martini glass. Squeeze
the lime wedge over the drink and add it as a garnish.

BARTENDER'S TIP
For an after-dinner drink, sprinkle with grated chocolate —
use dark, milk and white chocolate.

MOSCOW MULE

Seems docile enough, but beware the mighty kick.

ice cubes
45 ml (1$\frac{1}{2}$ oz) vodka
15 ml ($\frac{1}{2}$ oz) lime juice
non-alcoholic ginger beer
lime wedge

Half-fill a highball glass with ice. Add the vodka and lime juice, then top up with ginger beer and garnish with a wedge of lime.

— SEABREEZE —

Check the current, set your sails and let the ocean winds take you where they will.

ice cubes
45 ml (1¹/2 oz) vodka
60 ml (2 oz) cranberry juice
60 ml (2 oz) ruby red grapefruit juice
15 ml (¹/2 oz) lime juice
lime twist

Half-fill a cocktail shaker with ice. Add the vodka, cranberry juice, grapefruit juice and lime juice. Shake well and strain into a highball glass half-filled with ice. Garnish with a twist of lime.

—BISON KICK—

Bison grass has reputed aphrodisiac qualities —
for buffaloes at least. Who knows what a shot
or two might do for you?

ice cubes
45 ml (1^1/2 oz) bison grass vodka
10 ml (^{1}/4 oz) sake
30 ml (1 oz) watermelon juice
15 ml (^{1}/2 oz) lychee juice
10 ml (^{1}/4 oz) sugar syrup
1 peeled fresh lychee

Half-fill a cocktail shaker with ice. Add the vodka,
sake, watermelon juice, lychee juice and sugar syrup.
Shake vigorously and strain into a chilled cocktail
glass. Garnish with a lychee.

— SUZY WONG —

Too many of these and you'll be up at
the mike singing woozy songs.

ice cubes
45 ml (1¹/2 oz) citrus vodka
1 teaspoon lime juice
1 teaspoon sugar syrup
45 ml (1¹/2 oz) watermelon juice
lime twist

Fill a mixing glass with ice. Add the vodka, lime juice,
sugar syrup and watermelon juice. Stir, then strain into
a chilled cocktail glass. Garnish with a twist of lime.

NEGRONI

You either love it or hate it, but the bitterly complex
negroni has legion fans, having graced menus for
close to a century.

ice cubes
30 ml (1 oz) gin
30 ml (1 oz) sweet vermouth
30 ml (1 oz) Campari
soda water (optional)
orange twist

Half-fill a mixing glass with ice. Add the gin, vermouth
and Campari. Stir well, then strain into a chilled cocktail
glass. Add a dash of soda water if you wish. Garnish
with a twist of orange.

BERRY
COLLINS

The blueberry of happiness brightens up
old Tom's club lounge classic.

2 tablespoons blueberries
15 ml (1/2 oz) sugar syrup
ice cubes
45 ml (11/2 oz) gin
30 ml (1 oz) vanilla liqueur
15 ml (1/2 oz) lemon juice
cranberry juice or lemonade

Muddle the blueberries with the sugar syrup in a cocktail
shaker. Add a scoop of ice, then the gin, vanilla liqueur and
lemon juice. Shake vigorously and pour into a tall glass to
2.5 cm (1 inch) from the top, then top up with cranberry
juice or lemonade.

JUNGLE JUICE

Forget the concrete jungle, we're off to the rum jungle on a high-spirited cocktail safari, so grab your pith helmet and insect repellent and get ready for some wild nights, no passouts allowed. Just remember jungle potions have potent effects — imbibe too many and you might start seeing blue devils and pink elephants. Now turn the music up a notch, it's time to jungle boogie! Get down, get down …

FRUITY ADVENTURES

THIS IS A STORY ABOUT rambunctious rum runners, punch-happy persuaders, cool customers from the Caribbean and their Mexican mates — a gang of heavy-duty party troopers who know how to get things started! Their fiery, fruity prescriptions will rev up the action at the drop of a hat and inspire bouts of revelry and even devilry. Essential supplies for this bacchanalian adventure include rum aplenty, both dark and white, from standard to overproof intensity. Procure several bottles of tequila for slamming down some wicked margaritas, and a generous supply of gin and vodka. A few heady punches call for ingredients such as bubbly, red wine, Pimm's No. 1, bourbon and sweet vermouth. It's bound to get hot so keep buckets of ice on hand, as well as thirst quenchers such as tonic water (to fend off malaria), soda water, cola, lemonade and ginger ale. Deep in the jungle pluck a fresh harvest of limes, lemons, pineapple and oranges to squeeze into your drinks (you'll need your vitamin C). Other reviving essences include Angostura bitters, sugar syrup, fruit brandies and fruity liqueurs (blackcurrant, banana, strawberry, melon), amaretto, Cointreau, Grand Marnier, Galliano and the darkly mysterious Kahlúa. Blue curaçao, green Chartreuse, green crème de menthe and grenadine are the secret to the exquisite bird-of-paradise colours glimpsed in our potions, the likes of which are rarely seen. So let our journey begin.

PIMM'S PUNCH

Family celebrations call for a certain calibre of drink.
Here's something that will keep everybody happy.

375 ml (13 oz/1½ cups) orange juice
ice cubes
400 ml (14 oz) Pimm's No. 1
400 ml (14 oz) bourbon
185 ml (6 oz) sweet vermouth
185 ml (6 oz) white rum
1 bottle of Champagne or sparkling wine
3 cups chopped fresh fruit

Freeze 90 ml (3 oz) of the orange juice in an ice-cube tray.
Half-fill a punch bowl with ice, then add the Pimm's,
bourbon, vermouth, rum, remaining orange juice and the
Champagne or sparkling wine. Stir in the fresh fruit and
the frozen orange juice ice cubes.

SERVES 10.

BARTENDER'S TIP
Some people like to add mint leaves and cucumber slices.

SANGRIA

While away a lazy afternoon with a good pal
and a jug of fruity sangria.

15 ml (1/2 oz) lemon juice
15 ml (1/2 oz) orange juice
1 1/2 tablespoons caster (superfine) sugar
1 bottle of red wine
570 ml (20 oz) lemonade
45 ml (1 1/2 oz) gin
45 ml (1 1/2 oz) vodka
1 lemon
1 orange
1 lime
ice cubes

Put the lemon juice, orange juice and sugar in a large jug
or bowl and stir until the sugar has dissolved. Add the red
wine, lemonade, gin and vodka. Cut the lemon, orange and
lime in half, remove the seeds and slice finely. Add the
fruit to the jug, fill with ice, stir and serve.

SERVES 10.

MAI TAI

In Tahitian, *mai tai* roughly translates as 'out of this world'. After just one mai tai, you too will be out of this world.

crushed ice
30 ml (1 oz) white rum
30 ml (1 oz) dark rum
15 ml (1/2 oz) Cointreau
15 ml (1/2 oz) amaretto
15 ml (1/2 oz) lemon juice
90 ml (3 oz) pineapple juice
90 ml (3 oz) orange juice
15 ml (1/2 oz) sugar syrup
dash of grenadine
lime slice
mint leaves

Half-fill a large goblet glass with crushed ice. Add the white rum, dark rum, Cointreau, amaretto, lemon juice, pineapple juice, orange juice, sugar syrup and grenadine. Stir, then garnish with a slice of lime and some mint leaves.

— CUBA LIBRE —

Throw off the shackles, free your mind
and embrace the spirit of revolution.

ice cubes
60 ml (2 oz) white rum
6 lime wedges
cola
lime wedge

Half-fill a highball glass with ice. Add the rum,
squeeze the lime wedges into the glass, then add
the squeezed wedges to the drink. Top up with cola
and garnish with a wedge of lime.

MARGARITA

SHAKEN... Party people the world over know how to shake the place up. They're the ones wielding a shaken margarita.

2 lime wedges
salt
ice cubes
45 ml (1½ oz) tequila
15 ml (½ oz) Cointreau
15 ml (½ oz) lemon juice
15 ml (½ oz) lime juice
dash of sugar syrup

Run a wedge of lime around the rim of a cocktail glass. Dip the rim into a saucer of salt, shaking off any excess. Chill the glass. Half-fill a cocktail shaker with ice and add the tequila, Cointreau, lemon juice, lime juice and sugar syrup. Shake well, then strain into the salt-frosted cocktail glass. Garnish with the remaining wedge of lime.

BARTENDER'S TIP
To frost a cocktail glass, simply invert it by the neck, run a lime or lemon wedge around the rim, then dip the rim into a saucer of salt, shaking off any excess.

MARGARITA

FROZEN... For your next party trick, serve these up in shot glasses with the salt and lemon on the side.

2 lime wedges
salt
1 cup crushed ice
45 ml (1½ oz) tequila
15 ml (½ oz) Cointreau
15 ml (½ oz) lemon juice
15 ml (½ oz) lime juice
dash of sugar syrup

Run a wedge of lime around the rim of a cocktail glass. Dip the rim in a saucer of salt, shaking off any excess. Chill the glass. Place the crushed ice, tequila, Cointreau, lemon juice, lime juice and sugar syrup in a blender. Blend until the mixture is the consistency of shaved ice, pour into the salt-frosted cocktail glass and garnish with the remaining wedge of lime.

EL DIABLO

There's a little devil in all of us just yearning to be set free with a glass of sparkling potion.

ice cubes
60 ml (2 oz) tequila
30 ml (1 oz) blackcurrant liqueur
ginger ale
lime wedge

Half-fill an old-fashioned glass with ice, add the tequila and blackcurrant liqueur, then top up with ginger ale. Squeeze the lime wedge into the glass, and add the squeezed wedge to the drink. Stir.

FREDDIE
— FUDPUCKER —

Whatever you do, don't try to order another one of
these after you've finished the first.

ice cubes
45 ml (1½ oz) tequila
15 ml (½ oz) Galliano
60 ml (2 oz) orange juice
half an orange slice
maraschino cherry

Half-fill a cocktail shaker with ice. Add the tequila, Galliano
and orange juice, shake vigorously and strain into a chilled
cocktail glass. Garnish with half a slice of orange and a
maraschino cherry.

TEQUILA
SUNRISE

Sunrise can be a scary sight when you still have one
of these in your hand.

ice cubes
30 ml (1 oz) tequila
orange juice
dash of grenadine
orange twist

Half-fill a highball glass with ice. Add the tequila and top up
with orange juice. Add the grenadine by carefully pouring it
over the back of a spoon. Garnish with a twist of orange.

OLÉ

South of the border the party starts early and
finishes late. Celebrate with a local shout.

ice cubes
45 ml (1½ oz) tequila
30 ml (1 oz) banana liqueur
dash of blue curaçao

Half-fill a cocktail shaker with ice. Add the tequila and
banana liqueur, then shake well. Strain into a small, chilled
cocktail glass. Tip a dash of blue curaçao into the drink to
achieve a two-tone effect.

HARVEY
— WALLBANGER —

Whatever issues Harvey may have had with that
wall, it certainly resulted in a classic drop.

crushed ice
30 ml (1 oz) vodka
10 ml (1/4 oz) Galliano
orange juice
half an orange slice

Half-fill a highball glass with crushed ice. Add the vodka
and Galliano, then top up with orange juice. Garnish with
half a slice of orange.

CORPSE REVIVER

Stash this powerful medicine in your first aid kit and
reserve for an emergency kickstart.

ice cubes
30 ml (1 oz) brandy
30 ml (1 oz) Calvados
30 ml (1 oz) sweet vermouth
apple slices

Half-fill a cocktail shaker with ice. Add the brandy,
Calvados and vermouth, shake vigorously and strain
into a chilled cocktail glass. Garnish with apple slices.

FROU FROU

Frills and thrills galore for those fancying a little afternoon delight or a fleeting flirtation with sweetness and light. From the decadently opulent to the wildly whimsical, nothing here is to be taken too seriously. It's high time to flaunt it so frock up for a full-on fanfare. Flounce about in your flashiest feathers, primp and preen your prettiest peacock plumes and settle back for a fantasia on ice.

FANTASTICAL FANCIES

THIS CHAPTER COULD ALMOST be described as a midsummer night's dream. So let us introduce a tutti-frutti cast of players whose sole mission is to entice the senses and tickle the most fantastical of fancies — to utterly delight, indulge and entertain. What follows is a kaleidoscope of technicolour dreams featuring a vast, eclectic troop of royal luminaries such as Champagne, Cointreau, Pernod and Parfait Amour, cameo appearances by instantly recognizable types such as gin, vodka and white rum (clearly low-lifes!), a gamut of resplendent liqueurs (melon, peach, strawberry, banana and chocolate) — an ensemble superbly supported by notables such as amaretto, cherry brandy, Sambuca, Malibu, green crème de menthe, white crème de cacao and blue curaçao. Keeping up appearances is integral to the show, with many a flamboyant flourish anticipated from exotic fruits and maraschino cherries; expect juicy performances and an acerbic wit from limes, lemons and pineapples. Plot thickeners include agents as diverse as sugar syrup, rosewater, grenadine, Angostura bitters, raspberry cordial, lemonade and apple cider. And for comic relief, don't miss a rib-tickling appearance by a liquorice allsort and a jelly bean! All in all, a glittering show at once zany, capricious and wanton, guaranteed to make you feel for one tizzy, giddy moment gloriously and unashamedly *chi chi*.

So let the show begin …

CHAMPAGNE
— AND LYCHEE —
JELLY SHOTS

Greet the glitterati with these jewel-studded jelly shots and watch their jaws drop.

1 gelatine leaf
15 ml (1/2 oz) sugar syrup
120 ml (4 oz) Champagne or sparkling wine
3 lychees, peeled, seeded and halved
6 raspberries

Soak the gelatine in cold water. Heat the sugar syrup and Champagne or sparkling wine until just hot. Squeeze the liquid out of the gelatine, add the gelatine to the Champagne mixture and stir until dissolved. Cool, then place half a lychee and a raspberry into six shot glasses. Pour in the Champagne mixture and chill for 3 hours, or until set.

MAKES 6.

FRAPPÉ

Parfait Amour speaks in hushed tones of
simmering, ardent passions. In a frappé it
is a pure *frisson* of love.

crushed ice
15 ml (1/2 oz) Parfait Amour
15 ml (1/2 oz) Cointreau

Fill a large goblet with crushed ice, then pour over
the Parfait Amour and Cointreau. Serve with a short
straw or a long-handled spoon.

RASPBERRY
— CHAMPAGNE —
SPIDER

This magical version of a childhood classic could have slipped straight out of *Alice's Adventures in Wonderland*.

1–2 raspberry sorbet balls
chilled Champagne or sparkling wine

Place one or two balls of raspberry sorbet in a chilled champagne flute and slowly top up with Champagne or sparkling wine.

Bartender's Tip
Scoop a tub of raspberry sorbet into small balls with a melon baller and freeze until needed.

STRAWBERRY FLAPPER

Make like the bright young things of the
Roaring Twenties and dazzle the boys with
this snappy number.

4 hulled strawberries
4 ice cubes
15 ml (1/2 oz) strawberry liqueur
chilled Champagne or sparkling wine

Place the strawberries, ice cubes and strawberry liqueur
in a heavy-duty blender, then blend until smooth. Pour
into a chilled champagne flute and slowly top up with
Champagne or sparkling wine.

GRAPE MARTINI

These martinis are so damn lovely you could drink a whole bunch of them.

6 red grapes
6 white grapes
15 ml (1/2 oz) sugar syrup
ice cubes
60 ml (2 oz) vodka

Muddle five red and five white grapes with the sugar syrup in a cocktail shaker. Add a scoop of ice and the vodka. Shake vigorously and strain into a chilled martini glass. Garnish with the remaining red and white grapes on a wooden skewer.

WATERMELON AND
— ROSEWATER —
MARTINI

When the occasion calls for utter decadence
— and even when it doesn't.

5 chunks of watermelon
15 ml (½ oz) sugar syrup
ice cubes
60 ml (2 oz) watermelon-infused vodka
(see recipe on page 17)
3 drops of rosewater
3 rose petals

Muddle the watermelon with the sugar syrup in a cocktail
shaker. Add a scoop of ice, then the vodka and rosewater.
Shake vigorously and strain into a chilled martini glass.
Garnish with floating rose petals.

— RED BLOSSOM —

No-one will ever blow raspberries at this
bloomin' beautiful extravaganza.

ice cubes
45 ml (1 1/2 oz) gin
15 ml (1/2 oz) peach liqueur
2 tablespoons raspberries
15 ml (1/2 oz) lemon juice
15 ml (1/2 oz) sugar syrup
3 blueberries

Add a scoop of ice to a cocktail shaker, then the gin,
peach liqueur, raspberries, lemon juice and sugar
syrup. Shake vigorously and strain into a chilled martini
glass. Garnish with blueberries.

FALLEN ANGEL

Your halo may have slipped a little but this heavenly creation will give you wings.

ice cubes
45 ml (1½ oz) gin
15 ml (½ oz) green crème de menthe
30 ml (1 oz) lemon juice
dash of Angostura bitters
maraschino cherry

Half-fill a cocktail shaker with ice. Add the gin, crème de menthe, lemon juice and bitters, then shake vigorously. Strain into a chilled cocktail glass and garnish with a maraschino cherry.

JAPANESE
EGG NOG

East meets West in this sophisticated
fusion of egg and nog.

ice cubes
45 ml (1½ oz) Cointreau
45 ml (1½ oz) melon liqueur
80 ml (2½ oz) milk
dash of egg white

Half-fill a cocktail shaker with ice. Add the Cointreau,
melon liqueur, milk and egg white, then shake well.
Strain into a chilled cocktail glass.

JAPANESE SLIPPER

Reorient yourself and sip into something
really comforting.

ice cubes
30 ml (1 oz) melon liqueur
30 ml (1 oz) Cointreau
15 ml (1/2 oz) lemon juice
maraschino cherry

Half-fill a cocktail shaker with ice. Add the melon liqueur,
Cointreau and lemon juice. Shake well and strain into a
chilled cocktail glass. Garnish with a maraschino cherry.

SHAMPOO

Recommended for internal use only, this frothy
formulation is guaranteed to leave no tears.

15 ml (1/2 oz) gin
15 ml (1/2 oz) lemon juice
dash of Pernod
dash of blue curaçao
chilled Champagne or sparkling wine
lemon twist

Pour the gin, then the lemon juice, Pernod and
blue curaçao into a chilled champagne flute. Slowly
top up with Champagne or sparkling wine and
garnish with a twist of lemon.

TROPICANA

Imagine yourself in an equatorial loveland
sequestered from care, sipping like a giant
hummingbird on precious nectars extracted
from the rampant fruits of the warm wet
earth. Wear a flower in your hair and feel
the sensual island breeze caress your sun-
kissed cheeks. Marvel at the mighty sun's
slow trajectory through the sky and at its
fiery demise. This is the island time forgot.
Welcome to paradise.

GO TROPPO

WHEN THE ANTICS of this maddening world start to drive you bananas and make you lose your coconuts, you know you need to pack up your bongos and go troppo for a while. Extract yourself from the feverish melée and tune into island time, where life has a slower, stronger pulse and moves at a leisurely pace. Feel the slow crash of the surf on the beach, dig your toes deep into fine white squeaky-clean sand and then administer some strong tropical medicines such as rum and tequila in the form of a daiquiri, margarita or piña colada. For the full island experience, don't forget the Grand Marnier, Cointreau, Galliano, Malibu, Kahlúa and crème de cacao, and don't skimp on the cream, milk and coconut cream. The pounding sun and soaring mercury can challenge the equanimity, but mercifully this is an abundant place, where fruits and berries grow in jungly profusion to slake your thirst and keep you cool. Celebrate nature's bounty with fruity liqueurs and purées in a rainbow of flavours. Even our 'dear little water' vodka is infused with luscious essences — citrus, peach, vanilla and currants. Other essential requirements in this magical place are a cargo hold of cold, cold ice, cocktail umbrellas, a deckchair, sarong (or a grass skirt if you prefer), an outlandish pair of sunglasses, a flouncy broad-brimmed hat and a nice pair of lovely hands to rub some sunscreen into those out of the way spots. Aloha, heaven.

ORANGE
— JELLY SHOTS —

Make these in the prettiest shot glasses you can find!

1 gelatine leaf
15 ml (1/2 oz) sugar syrup
80 ml (2 1/2 oz) pulp-free orange juice
15 ml (1/2 oz) lemon juice
60 ml (2 oz) Grand Marnier
15 ml (1/2 oz) Galliano
6 orange segments

Soak the gelatine leaf in cold water. Heat the sugar syrup,
orange juice and lemon juice until just hot. Squeeze the
liquid out of the gelatine, add the gelatine to the juice
mixture and stir until dissolved. Cool, then add the
Grand Marnier and Galliano. Place an orange segment
in six shot glasses and pour in the juice mixture.
Refrigerate for 3 hours, or until set.

MAKES 6.

DAIQUIRIS

SHAKEN... Take it shaken and you may find yourself well stirred.

ice cubes
45 ml (1½ oz) white rum
30 ml (1 oz) lime juice
15 ml (½ oz) sugar syrup

Half-fill a cocktail shaker with ice. Add the rum, lime juice and sugar syrup. Shake vigorously and strain into a chilled cocktail glass.

FROZEN... A memorable way to melt the ice — better make it in bulk.

1 cup crushed ice
45 ml (1½ oz) white rum
30 ml (1 oz) lime juice
15 ml (½ oz) sugar syrup
lime twist

Place the crushed ice, rum, lime juice and sugar syrup in a blender and blend until the mixture is the consistency of shaved ice. Pour into a chilled cocktail glass and garnish with a twist of lime.

PINEAPPLE, LYCHEE AND MINT DAIQUIRI

The fragrant sweetness of lychees lifts the humble
daiquiri into the realms of legend.

4 mint leaves
45 ml (1½ oz) white rum
80 g (2½ oz/½ cup) diced fresh pineapple
4 lychees, peeled and seeded
15 ml (½ oz) pineapple juice
15 ml (½ oz) lime juice
15 ml (½ oz) sugar syrup
1 cup crushed ice
pineapple leaves
mint sprig

Place the mint, rum, pineapple, lychees, pineapple juice,
lime juice and sugar syrup in a blender. Add the crushed
ice and blend until the mixture is the consistency of
shaved ice. Pour into a large chilled cocktail glass and
garnish with pineapple leaves and a sprig of mint.

PASSIONFRUIT AND −VANILLA VODKA− JELLY SHOTS

A tempting taste of paradise in every tiny shot.

1 gelatine leaf
15 ml ($1/2$ oz) sugar syrup
80 ml ($21/2$ oz) passionfruit pulp
80 ml ($21/2$ oz) vanilla vodka

Soak the gelatine leaf in cold water. Heat the sugar syrup and passionfruit pulp until just hot. Squeeze the liquid out of the gelatine, add the gelatine to the passionfruit mixture and stir to dissolve. Cool, stir in the vodka and pour into six shot glasses. Refrigerate for 3 hours, or until set.

MAKES 6.

BLOOD ORANGE
— MARGARITA —

Any time you want to impress the pants off
somebody wow them with this awesomely
mesmerizing margarita.

egg white
caster (superfine) sugar
ice cubes
45 ml (1$\frac{1}{2}$ oz) gold tequila
15 ml ($\frac{1}{2}$ oz) Mandarine Napoleon or Grand Marnier
15 ml ($\frac{1}{2}$ oz) lime juice
30 ml (1 oz) blood orange juice
10 ml ($\frac{1}{4}$ oz) sugar syrup

Dip the rim of a cocktail glass in a saucer of egg white,
then a saucer of sugar, shaking off any excess. Chill. Add
a scoop of ice to a cocktail shaker, then the tequila,
Mandarine Napoleon or Grand Marnier, lime juice, blood
orange juice and sugar syrup. Shake vigorously and strain
into the sugar-frosted cocktail glass.

STRAWBERRY
— MARGARITA —

Pretty in pink with a lemon–lime surprise, this
sublime cocktail will smoothe over any rough patch.

lemon wedge

salt

crushed ice

30 ml (1 oz) tequila

15 ml (1/2 oz) strawberry liqueur

15 ml (1/2 oz) Cointreau

15 ml (1/2 oz) sugar syrup

15 ml (1/2 oz) lemon juice

strawberry half

lemon slice

Run a lemon wedge around the rim of a cocktail glass.
Dip the rim into a saucer of salt and chill. Blend the
crushed ice, tequila, strawberry liqueur, Cointreau,
sugar syrup and lemon juice in a blender and pour into
the salt-frosted cocktail glass. Garnish with a strawberry
half and a slice of lemon.

KIWI
— MARGARITA —

Take a flight of fancy to the land of the
long white cloud.

egg white
caster (superfine) sugar
crushed ice
45 ml (1½ oz) tequila
15 ml (½ oz) Cointreau
15 ml (½ oz) melon liqueur
15 ml (½ oz) lemon juice
1–2 kiwifruit, peeled and chopped
kiwifruit slice

Dip the rim of a cocktail glass in a saucer of egg white,
then a saucer of sugar, shaking off any excess. Chill.
Place the crushed ice, tequila, Cointreau, melon liqueur,
lemon juice and kiwifruit in a blender and blend well.
Pour into the sugar-frosted cocktail glass and garnish
with a slice of kiwifruit.

PASSIONFRUIT
— MARGARITA —

Resuscitate a flagging romance with
a passionate fling.

egg white
caster (superfine) sugar
ice cubes
45 ml (1½ oz) gold tequila
10 ml (¼ oz) Cointreau
30 ml (1 oz) passionfruit purée
15 ml (½ oz) lemon juice
15 ml (½ oz) lime juice
10 ml (¼ oz) sugar syrup

Dip the rim of a cocktail glass in a saucer of egg white,
then a saucer of sugar, shaking off any excess. Chill.
Add a scoop of ice to a cocktail shaker, then the tequila,
Cointreau, passionfruit purée, lemon juice, lime juice
and sugar syrup. Shake vigorously and strain into the
sugar-rimmed cocktail glass.

ILLUSION

When the master of illusion strikes,
clear your vision with a charge of this.

ice cubes
15 ml (1/2 oz) melon liqueur
15 ml (1/2 oz) Cointreau
15 ml (1/2 oz) vodka
15 ml (1/2 oz) lemon juice
15 ml (1/2 oz) pineapple juice
pineapple leaves

Half-fill a cocktail shaker with ice. Add the melon liqueur,
Cointreau, vodka, lemon juice and pineapple juice. Shake
vigorously and strain into a chilled cocktail glass. Garnish
with pineapple leaves.

DIABLO

When the temperature starts getting hellishly
hot, here's a diabolically refreshing diversion
for blasted palates.

ice cubes
45 ml (1½ oz) currant vodka
30 ml (1 oz) blackberry liqueur
30 ml (1 oz) pineapple juice
pineapple leaf

Add a scoop of ice to a cocktail shaker, then the vodka,
blackberry liqueur and pineapple juice. Shake vigorously
and strain into a chilled martini glass. Garnish with
a pineapple leaf.

SEX ON THE
BEACH

No sand, no insects, no seaweed. This has to be better than the real thing!

ice cubes
45 ml (1 1/2 oz) vodka
15 ml (1/2 oz) peach schnapps
45 ml (1 1/2 oz) pineapple juice
45 ml (1 1/2 oz) cranberry juice
crushed ice

Half-fill a cocktail shaker with ice. Add the vodka, schnapps, pineapple juice and cranberry juice and shake well. Strain into a tall cocktail glass half-filled with crushed ice.

HAVANA
SPECIAL

A capital drink capturing the balmy breezes,
vibrant life and vivid colours of Cuba.

ice cubes
60 ml (2 oz) pineapple juice
10 ml (1/4 oz) cherry brandy
45 ml (1½ oz) white rum
stemmed cocktail cherry

Half-fill a cocktail shaker with ice. Add the pineapple juice,
cherry brandy and rum. Shake vigorously and strain into
a cocktail glass half-filled with ice. Garnish with a stemmed
cocktail cherry.

BARBADOS
FONDUE

A fantasy island adventure in a tumbler.

half a lime, chopped
half a mango, peeled
6 small chunks of young coconut flesh
15 ml (½ oz) sugar syrup
ice cubes
45 ml (1½ oz) peach-infused vodka
(see recipe on page 17)
30 ml (1 oz) guava juice
strawberry half

Muddle the lime, mango and coconut with the sugar syrup
in a cocktail shaker. Add a scoop of ice, then the vodka and
guava juice. Shake vigorously, pour into a chilled tumbler
and garnish with half a strawberry.

—PIÑA COLADA—

This really should be drunk out of a hollowed-out
pineapple, and preferably in the shallow
end of a pool!

1 cup crushed ice
45 ml (1½ oz) white rum
15 ml (½ oz) coconut cream
15 ml (½ oz) Malibu rum
100 ml (3½ oz) pineapple juice
15 ml (½ oz) sugar syrup
pineapple leaves

Place the crushed ice, rum, coconut cream, Malibu,
pineapple juice and sugar syrup in a blender and blend
until the mixture is the consistency of shaved ice. Pour
into a large, chilled cocktail glass and garnish with
pineapple leaves and a cocktail umbrella.

— COCO COLADA —

Unfurl an umbrella, spread out a towel, purloin a
couple of coconuts and stake out your own little
corner of the Caribbean.

45 ml (1½ oz) brown crème de cacao
125 ml (4 oz/½ cup) pineapple juice
45 ml (1½ oz) coconut cream
crushed ice
pineapple wedge

Place the crème de cacao, pineapple juice, coconut cream
and some crushed ice in a blender and blend until smooth.
Pour into a large, chilled cocktail glass and garnish
with a pineapple wedge.

CHI CHI

San Tropez is so very far from here, but with
this chic number a Riviera moment is just
a swizzle stick away.

crushed ice
45 ml (1$^{1}/_{2}$ oz) vodka
15 ml ($^{1}/_{2}$ oz) Malibu rum
15 ml ($^{1}/_{2}$ oz) coconut cream
125 ml (4 oz/$^{1}/_{2}$ cup) pineapple juice
pineapple wedge
strawberry slices

Place some crushed ice, the vodka, Malibu rum, coconut
cream and pineapple juice in a blender and blend well.
Pour into a large, chilled tumbler and garnish with a small
wedge of pineapple and strawberry slices.

MUDDLED

It isn't always such a bad thing to feel a little muddled. Indeed, a muddled cocktail is a wonderful thing! The drinks in this chapter draw their inspiration from exotic corners of the globe, seeking out wild combinations of delirious new flavours to baffle the tongue, awaken the tastebuds and send your senses spinning. It's only natural to feel a little disoriented. Follow your nose and you'll be fine …

FEISTY, FIERY, FRESH

IT ALL BEGAN INNOCENTLY ENOUGH, as excellent adventures often do. Someone muddled and mashed and ground and gently bashed some fruit and herbs around in a cocktail shaker, releasing a burst of powerfully fresh flavours into our tired old drinks, instantly firing up our fatigued palates. Suddenly we were bounding about in Chile, or was it Peru, sampling copious amounts of pisco, a clear, brandy-like spirit that both countries claim as their national drink. Who are we to argue? Next stop Brazil, where we took on board some cachaça, a sterling distillation of unrefined sugarcane juice roughly translating as 'farmer's drink'. But it was only when somebody muddled some kiwifruit and ginger into their caipiroska that things started getting really confusing! Sometime around sunset we cruised off into the Caribbean for some crazy mojitos, then meandered down Mexico way to sample a little gold tequila, simultaneously stumbling upon some wondrous new tequilas spiked with vanilla, chilli and cinnamon! After our feisty, fiery Latino lovers we happily surrendered to a strangely sweet Oriental intrigue, seduced by wildly wonderful vodkas tasting of lemon grass, citrus, cinnamon and honey, with a dash of mint-infused dry vermouth, and flavours crushed from citrus, coriander (cilantro), cucumber, tamarillo, blood orange and lemon grass. Where we are now, nobody knows, but life will never be the same again.

MOJITO

This Cuban classic is sure to get your mojo going. But first a word of warning: they're supernaturally addictive!

8 mint leaves
half a lime, chopped
15 ml (1/2 oz) sugar syrup
ice cubes
60 ml (2 oz) white rum
soda water

Muddle the mint and lime with the sugar syrup in a cocktail shaker. Add a scoop of ice, then the rum. Shake vigorously and strain into a chilled tumbler 2.5 cm (1 inch) from the top, then top up with soda water.

CORIANDER
—————— MOJITO ——————

Coriander in a cocktail? Sounds a little cuckoo, but
try it once and you'll be stalking another.

1 handful coriander (cilantro)
1 lime, chopped
1 teaspoon sugar
15 ml (1/2 oz) sugar syrup
ice cubes
60 ml (2 oz) white rum
soda water

Muddle the coriander and lime with the sugar and sugar
syrup in a cocktail shaker. Add a scoop of ice, then the
rum. Shake vigorously and strain into a chilled tumbler
2.5 cm (1 inch) from the top, then top up with soda water.

— CAIPIROSKA —

A caipirinha made from vodka rather than cachaça.
Boy, those Brazilians sure know how to create a
carnival atmosphere!

1 lime, chopped
3 teaspoons caster (superfine) sugar
15 ml (1/2 oz) sugar syrup
ice cubes
60 ml (2 oz) vodka

Muddle the lime with the sugar and sugar syrup in
a cocktail shaker. Add a scoop of ice and the vodka.
Shake vigorously and strain into a chilled tumbler.
Serve with a chunk of lime.

BARTENDER'S TIP
You could make a minty caipiroska by muddling eight mint
leaves with the limes, sugar and sugar syrup.

— PISCO SOUR —

Make like an ancient and celebrate the spirit of South America with the national drink of Chile and Peru.

ice cubes
15 ml (^{1}/$_2$ oz) lemon juice
10 ml (^{1}/$_4$ oz) sugar syrup
45 ml (1^1/$_2$ oz) pisco
maraschino cherry

Half-fill a cocktail shaker with ice. Add the lemon juice, sugar syrup and pisco, then shake well. Strain into a chilled sour glass and garnish with a maraschino cherry.

LAMBADA
LICK

When lambada rhythms start to play, slurp, suck or
lick one of these and start to sway.

half a peach, chopped
30 ml (1 oz) passionfruit purée
15 ml (1/2 oz) sugar syrup
ice cubes
45 ml (1 1/2 oz) cachaça
dash of lime juice

Muddle the peach and passionfruit purée with the sugar
syrup in a cocktail shaker. Add a scoop of ice, then the
cachaça and lime juice. Shake vigorously and strain into
a chilled tumbler.

ACAPULCO GOLD

The sparkling riches gleaming within may prove
irresistibly alluring. Get out your shovel
and start digging.

1 lemon, chopped
15 ml (1/2 oz) sugar syrup
ice cubes
45 ml (1 1/2 oz) chilli-infused tequila
(see recipe on page 17)
15 ml (1/2 oz) vanilla liqueur
lemonade

Muddle the lemon and sugar syrup in a cocktail shaker.
Add a scoop of ice, then the tequila and vanilla liqueur.
Shake vigorously and strain into a tall, chilled glass 2.5 cm
(1 inch) from the top, then top up with lemonade.

EL HOMBRE

Will bring even the proudest man to his knees.

half a lemon, chopped
30 ml (1 oz) peach purée (see recipe on page 16)
15 ml (1/2 oz) sugar syrup
ice cubes
45 ml (11/2 oz) vanilla-infused tequila
(see recipe on page 17)
15 ml (1/2 oz) peach liqueur

Muddle the lemon and peach purée with the sugar syrup
in a cocktail shaker. Add a scoop of ice, then the tequila
and peach liqueur. Shake vigorously and strain into a
chilled tumbler.

MATADOR

Whip one of these out of your cape whenever you
need a flash of panache or a shot of brazen courage.

ice cubes
45 ml (1$\frac{1}{2}$ oz) cinnamon-infused tequila
(see recipe on page 17)
15 ml ($\frac{1}{2}$ oz) apple schnapps
15 ml ($\frac{1}{2}$ oz) lemon juice
30 ml (1 oz) apple juice
15 ml ($\frac{1}{2}$ oz) sugar syrup
thin apple slice

Half-fill a cocktail shaker with ice. Add the tequila,
schnapps, lemon juice, apple juice and sugar syrup.
Shake vigorously and strain into a chilled martini glass.
Garnish with a slice of apple.

SEÑORITA

Destined to stir the passions of any
hot-blooded woman.

1 tablespoon raspberries
1 tablespoon blueberries
15 ml ($\frac{1}{2}$ oz) sugar syrup
ice cubes
45 ml ($1\frac{1}{2}$ oz) gold tequila
15 ml ($\frac{1}{2}$ oz) raspberry liqueur
30 ml (1 oz) cranberry juice
lime wedge

Muddle the raspberries and blueberries with the sugar
syrup in a cocktail shaker. Add a scoop of ice, then the
tequila and raspberry liqueur. Shake vigorously and strain
into a chilled tumbler 2.5 cm (1 inch) from the top, then
top up with cranberry juice. Garnish with a wedge of lime.

—MATCHMAKER—

Love makes the world go round, but matchmakers
make the love go round.

1 tamarillo, chopped
8 mint leaves
15 ml (1/2 oz) sugar syrup
ice cubes
45 ml (1 1/2 oz) honey vodka
15 ml (1/2 oz) cinnamon-infused vodka
(see recipe on page 17)
10 ml (1/4 oz) lime juice
orange twist

Muddle the tamarillo and mint with the sugar syrup in a
cocktail shaker. Add a scoop of ice, then the two vodkas
and lime juice. Shake vigorously and strain into a chilled
martini glass. Garnish with a twist of orange.

BLOOD
SUNSET

To witness a blood sunset in all its glory can be a
rather intoxicating experience.

3 strawberries, halved
half a blood orange, chopped
15 ml (1/2 oz) sugar syrup
ice cubes
45 ml (11/2 oz) vodka
dash of lime juice

Muddle the strawberries and blood orange with the sugar
syrup in a cocktail shaker. Add a scoop of ice, then the
vodka and lime juice. Shake vigorously and pour into a
chilled tumbler.

ZOOT SUIT

Jump into your zaniest costume and you'll really
start to dig this outlandishly colourful outfit.

half an orange, chopped
half a lime, chopped
15 ml (1/2 oz) sugar syrup
ice cubes
45 ml (1½ oz) Campari
30 ml (1 oz) blood orange juice

Muddle the orange and lime with the sugar syrup in
a cocktail shaker. Add a scoop of ice, then the Campari
and blood orange juice. Shake vigorously and strain
into a chilled tumbler.

LEMON GRASS
—— MARTINI ——

For a crash course in Eastern philosophy,
meditate on this.

ice cubes
60 ml (2 oz) lemon grass-infused vodka
(see recipe on page 17)
15 ml (1/2 oz) ginger liqueur
15 ml (1/2 oz) sugar syrup
1 makrut (kaffir) lime leaf or lime twist

Half-fill a cocktail shaker with ice. Add the vodka, ginger
liqueur and sugar syrup. Shake vigorously and strain into
a chilled martini glass. Garnish with a lime leaf or
twist of lime.

— CAIPIRINHA —

Start your party with a round of Brazil's finest export
and you'll mardi gras all the way to Rio.

1 lime, chopped
3 teaspoons caster (superfine) sugar
15 ml (1/2 oz) sugar syrup
ice cubes
60 ml (2 oz) cachaça
mint sprig

Muddle the lime with the sugar and sugar syrup
in a cocktail shaker. Add a scoop of ice and the cachaça.
Shake vigorously, strain into a chilled tumbler and garnish
with a sprig of mint.

MINT AND
— CUCUMBER —
MARTINI

The coolest drink in the world just got cooler.

8 cucumber slices
10 mint leaves
10 ml (1/4 oz) sugar syrup
ice cubes
70 ml (21/4 oz) gin
10 ml (1/4 oz) mint-infused dry vermouth
(see recipe on page 17)
2 cucumber batons

Muddle the cucumber and mint with the sugar syrup
in a cocktail shaker. Add a scoop of ice, then the gin.
Coat the inside of a chilled martini glass with the
vermouth. Place a small sieve over the martini glass and
strain the martini into the glass. (This is known as double
straining, which ensures a lovely clear drink.) Garnish
with two cucumber batons.

CLUB LOUNGE

After a long, hard day spent engaged in strictly masculine pursuits, it was customary for men of good breeding to unwind in the rarefied ambience of the nineteenth hole, otherwise known as the gentleman's bar. In this world away from women, the man about town was free to indulge in a little dignified swilling of a clutch of classic drinks. All good sport, really. Who could blame them?

BOY'S OWN WORLD

STAKE YOUR PLACE ON a dark leather chesterfield and sink down into a boys' own world where topics of great import and jocularity are mulled over at leisure, tall tales are traded and deals are done over a card game and a drink or three. Settle back as the shadows lengthen from late in the afternoon until deep into the evening. Perhaps Sir would care to begin with a few afternoon refreshments, a sundowner or an appetite-provoking aperitif? We venture to suggest Sir might also wish to sample some appealing classics mixed from gin and vodka, or perhaps some relaxing brandy-based drinks, or if Sir has had a very rugged day he might prefer to proceed directly to our straight-talkin', sharp-shootin', hard-hitting, no-nonsense types such as whisky or bourbon. And when the business of the day is done, Sir may wish to sample a little snifter of late-night, top-shelf liqueurs such as cognac, Drambuie and Bénédictine.
A word to the wise bar manager: invest in some Pimm's No. 1, Campari, amaretto and vermouth, stock up on lemon, orange, grapefruit and tomato juice and mixers such as soda water, ginger ale and lemonade, and check your supplies of bitters, Tabasco, Worcestershire, lime juice cordial, grenadine and sugar syrup. Naturally, our garnishes are free of feminizing influences: a maraschino cherry is as fancy as it gets, but the usual adornments are slices of lemon, orange, cucumber with the odd celery stalk. Remember, discretion is the key …

PIMM'S

A British institution, Pimm's No. 1 is the commercial version of a gin sling, traditionally taken after a spot of tennis or golf.

ice cubes
45 ml (1½ oz) Pimm's No. 1
lemonade
ginger ale
slice of cucumber skin
orange slice
lemon slice

Half-fill a highball glass with ice. Add the Pimm's, then top up with lemonade and ginger ale. Garnish with slices of cucumber, orange and lemon.

— AMERICANO —

In the Prohibition years, this drink was freely
enjoyed as a 'medicinal' compound. James Bond
was also partial to a few.

ice cubes
15 ml (1/2 oz) Campari
15 ml (1/2 oz) sweet vermouth
soda water
orange slice
lemon slice

Half-fill an old-fashioned glass with ice. Add the Campari
and vermouth, then top up with soda water. Garnish with
slices of orange and lemon and serve with a swizzle stick.

SINGAPORE SLING

Created around the eve of World War I, this is the drink that made Singapore's Raffles Hotel famous.

ice cubes
45 ml (1 1/2 oz) gin
15 ml (1/2 oz) Bénédictine
15 ml (1/2 oz) Cointreau
15 ml (1/2 oz) cherry brandy
30 ml (1 oz) orange juice
30 ml (1 oz) pineapple juice
dash of lime juice
dash of grenadine
maraschino cherry

Half-fill a cocktail shaker with ice. Add all the ingredients except for the garnish, then shake well and strain into a tall glass half-filled with ice. Garnish with a maraschino cherry.

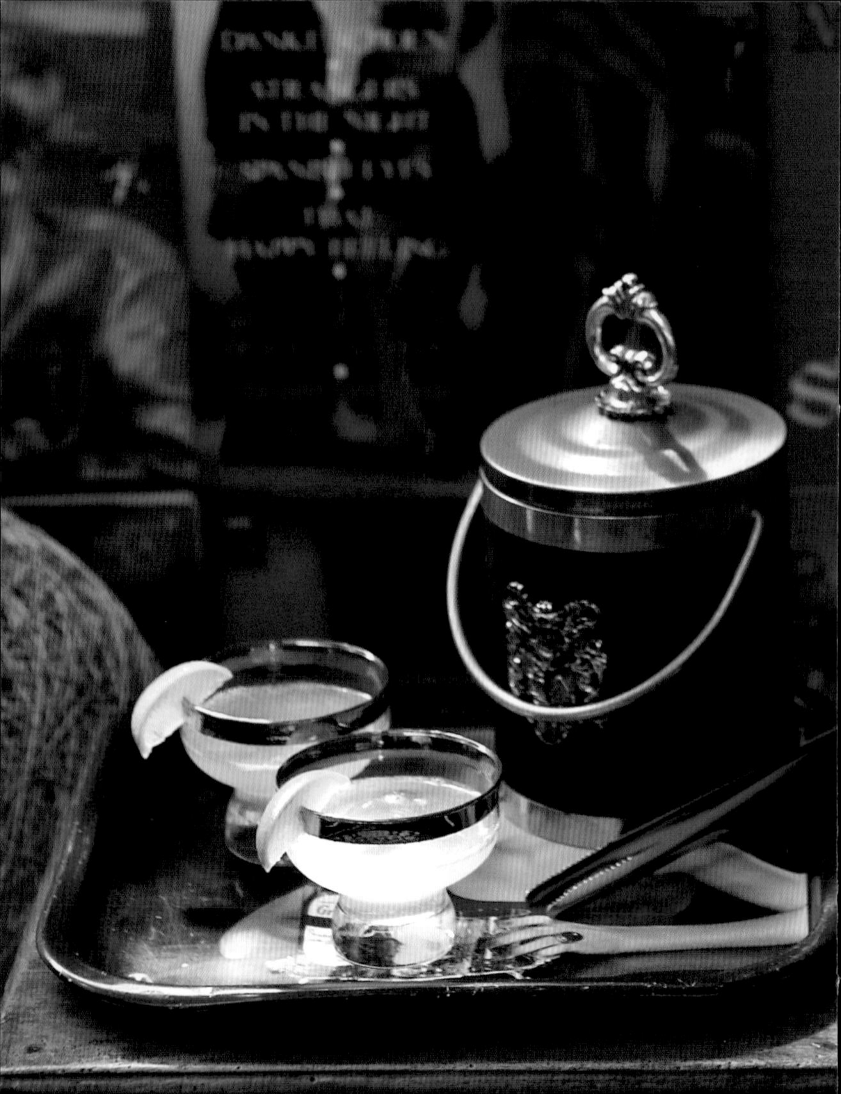

GIMLET

Steel your resolve and face the world with a gimlet eye. At the very least you'll ward off scurvy.

ice cubes
45 ml (1½ oz) gin
15 ml (½ oz) lime juice
15 ml (½ oz) lime juice cordial
lime twist
lime wedge

Half-fill a mixing glass with ice. Add the gin, lime juice and lime juice cordial and stir well. Strain into a chilled goblet and garnish with a twist of lime and a wedge of lime.

— SCREWDRIVER —

Everyone should have one of these in their toolbox
— you never know when you might need it.

ice cubes
45 ml (1¹/₂ oz) vodka
orange juice
maraschino cherry
orange twist

Three-quarters fill a highball glass with ice. Add the vodka
and top up with orange juice. Garnish with a maraschino
cherry and a twist of orange and serve with a straw.

SLOW
— COMFORTABLE —
SCREW

Only warm familiarity and years of shared memories
can take you down this long and winding road.

ice cubes
15 ml (1/2 oz) vodka
15 ml (1/2 oz) gin
15 ml (1/2 oz) Southern Comfort
orange juice
orange twist

Three-quarters fill a highball glass with ice. Add the vodka,
gin and Southern Comfort. Stir, top up with orange juice
and garnish with a twist of orange.

— BLOODY MARY —

Traditionally used as a 'hair of the dog', this invigorating tonic is too good to save for the morning after.

3 ice cubes
45 ml (1½ oz) vodka
4 drops of Tabasco sauce
1 teaspoon Worcestershire sauce
10 ml (¼ oz) lemon juice
pinch of salt
1 grind of black pepper
60 ml (2 oz) chilled tomato juice
1 crisp celery stalk

Place the ice cubes in a highball glass, pour in the vodka, then add the Tabasco, Worcestershire sauce and lemon juice. Add the salt and pepper, then pour in the tomato juice and stir well. Allow to sit for a minute, then garnish with a stalk of celery.

BARTENDER'S TIP
For extra zing, you could garnish your drink with wedges of lemon and lime.

LONG ISLAND
— ICED TEA —

A classy beverage, but not for high tea.
Just remember, one is a potent social lubricant,
two will knock you off your trolley.

ice cubes
15 ml (1/2 oz) white rum
15 ml (1/2 oz) vodka
15 ml (1/2 oz) gin
15 ml (1/2 oz) Cointreau
15 ml (1/2 oz) tequila
1/2 teaspoon lime juice
cola
lime wedge

Half-fill a highball glass with ice. Add the rum, vodka, gin,
Cointreau, tequila and lime juice, then top up with cola.
Stir well with a swizzle stick and garnish with a
wedge of lime.

SIDECAR

Swing out, sister, and travel in style — just remember to pack your goggles because it might be a long, cool ride.

ice cubes
30 ml (1 oz) brandy
15 ml (1/2 oz) Cointreau
30 ml (1 oz) lemon juice
lemon twist

Half-fill a cocktail shaker with ice. Add the brandy, Cointreau and lemon juice, then shake well. Strain into a chilled cocktail glass and garnish with a twist of lemon.

— MINT JULEP —

After a long, hot and sultry day, here's something
tall, cool and soothing to settle your sulky
southern belle.

ice cubes
60 ml (2 oz) bourbon
8 mint leaves
15 ml (1/2 oz) sugar syrup
dash of dark rum or brandy
mint sprig

Half-fill a mixing glass with ice. Add the bourbon, mint and
sugar, then stir. Strain into a highball glass filled with ice
and stir gently until the glass becomes frosted. Top with a
dash of rum or brandy. Garnish with a sprig of mint and
serve with a long straw.

BARTENDER'S TIP
Some people like to add a few chunks of cucumber
for extra refreshment.

— HIGHBALL —

Whether you want to get high or just have a ball,
this drink lives up to its name.

ice cubes
45 ml (1½ oz) rye whiskey
soda water or ginger ale
lemon twist

Half-fill a highball glass with ice. Add the rye whiskey and
top up with soda water or ginger ale. Garnish with
a twist of lemon.

WHISKEY SOUR

There's nothing quite like a brisk tumbler in the rye.

ice cubes
45 ml (1$\frac{1}{2}$ oz) rye whiskey
15 ml ($\frac{1}{2}$ oz) Cointreau
15 ml ($\frac{1}{2}$ oz) lemon juice
15 ml ($\frac{1}{2}$ oz) sugar syrup
maraschino cherry

Half-fill a cocktail shaker with ice. Add the rye whiskey,
Cointreau, lemon juice and sugar syrup, then shake well.
Strain into a tumbler and garnish with a maraschino cherry.

—NEW YORKER—

Cities don't come bigger than the Big Apple, and
drinks don't come classier than this.

ice cubes
45 ml (1 1/2 oz) rye whiskey
1 teaspoon lime juice
dash of grenadine
orange twist

Half-fill a cocktail shaker with ice. Add the rye whiskey,
lime juice and grenadine. Shake well, strain into a cocktail
glass and garnish with a twist of orange.

– OLD FASHIONED –

Slow down, sonny, pull up a chair, linger awhile
and reflect on days gone by.

1 sugar cube
dash of Angostura bitters
soda water
ice cubes
60 ml (2 oz) bourbon
orange twist (optional)

Place the sugar cube in an old-fashioned glass. Add the
bitters and let it soak into the sugar. Add a splash of soda
water and enough ice to half-fill the glass. Pour in the
bourbon and stir to dissolve the sugar. Garnish with a twist
of orange if you wish.

— GODFATHER —

A supremely powerful entity demanding
the utmost respect.

ice cubes
45 ml (1¹/2 oz) Scotch whisky
15 ml (¹/2 oz) amaretto

Fill an old-fashioned glass with ice, then build the
whisky and amaretto in the glass.

— GODMOTHER —

Who needs a magic wand when you have
one of these?

ice cubes
45 ml (1½ oz) vodka
15 ml (½ oz) amaretto

Fill an old-fashioned glass with ice, then build the vodka
and amaretto in the glass.

— RUSTY NAIL —

Hit the nail on the head with this hammer of a drink.

ice cubes
45 ml (1½ oz) Scotch whisky
45 ml (1½ oz) Drambuie
half an orange slice

Half-fill an old-fashioned tumbler with ice. Add the whisky
and Drambuie, then garnish with half a slice of orange.

MELLOW

Creamy, milky, sweet and dreamy, these cocktails are surely sent from high above to melt away the cares of the mortal day. At the end of a meal, these mellifluous offerings are like manna from heaven, delivering to all good people their just desserts, radiating smiles of deep contentment and a warm inner glow. Soothing and sublime, they are the supreme indulgence. Go on, you *know* you want to …

SUGAR AND SPICE

THIS CHAPTER HAS SPECIAL MEANING for people who are blessed with a pronounced predilection for creamy concoctions infused with sugar and spice and all things nice. This is the chapter where liqueurs are in their element, where Heaven meets Earth, and angels sing high up in the firmament (you might need to sip a few liqueurs to hear them). The word 'liqueur' derives from the Latin meaning to melt, or to dissolve — a very accurate description of their mellowing effects upon the human body. Liqueurs have been around for centuries and it seems they are now available in every conceivable flavour from fruity and herbal through to coffee and chocolatey. Just as well really. And while they can be combined in innumerable ways, the liqueurs you'll find keep cropping up in the most popular of our mellow cocktails include Frangelico, Irish Cream, Cointreau, Grand Marnier, Galliano, Tia Maria, Kahlúa, chocolate liqueur, advocaat and crème de cacao, and divine fruit liqueurs such as strawberry, melon and raspberry. Which is not to say you have to buy them all to be the consummate host — but then again, who's to stop you? Other valued friends from the spirit world that make their influence keenly felt here include gin, vodka and brandy, with special dispensation given to indulge in milk, cream, chocolate syrup, chocolate, freshly grated nutmeg, crushed hazelnuts, coffee, cloves and cinnamon.

Why delay? Life is short!

BRANDY
— ALEXANDER —

Who was Alexander? Who cares? But could
somebody pour the man a drink?

ice cubes
30 ml (1 oz) brandy
15 ml (1/2 oz) brown crème de cacao
30 ml (1 oz) cream
freshly grated nutmeg

Half-fill a cocktail shaker with ice. Add the brandy, crème
de cacao and cream, and shake vigorously. Strain into
a chilled cocktail glass and dust with nutmeg sprinkled
over two crossed straws.

EGG NOG PUNCH

No need to bother with dinner. A bowl of this will fill you up and warm the cockles of your heart.

5 eggs, separated
300 g (10$\frac{1}{2}$ oz) sugar
250 ml (9 oz/1 cup) bourbon
250 ml (9 oz/1 cup) cream
200 ml (7 oz) milk
freshly grated nutmeg

Whisk the egg whites until stiff, then slowly add a third of the sugar, whisking constantly until glossy. In a large serving bowl, beat the egg yolks with a third of the sugar until the sugar has dissolved. Slowly add the bourbon, whisking well. In another bowl, lightly whisk the cream with the remaining sugar until the sugar has dissolved. Gently fold the egg whites into the yolk mix, then fold in the cream. Slowly stir in the milk, then chill for 4 hours. Serve each glass dusted with a little grated nutmeg.

SERVES 10.

FRANKIE

Frankly, my dear, after several of these you certainly
will not give a damn.

ice cubes
15 ml (1/2 oz) Frangelico
15 ml (1/2 oz) Kahlúa
30 ml (1 oz) Irish Cream
30 ml (1 oz) cream
very finely crushed hazelnuts

Half-fill a cocktail shaker with ice. Add the Frangelico,
Kahlúa, Irish Cream and cream. Shake vigorously, then
strain into a large chilled cocktail glass. Serve sprinkled
with very finely crushed hazelnuts.

B 52

Clear the bar, line 'em up and bombs away, baby.

15 ml (1/2 oz) Kahlúa
15 ml (1/2 oz) Irish Cream
15 ml (1/2 oz) Cointreau

Pour the Kahlúa into a shot glass, then carefully float
the Irish Cream on top by pouring it over the back of a
teaspoon. Using a clean teaspoon, float the Cointreau
over the Irish Cream so you have three distinct layers.

— MALT MAFIA —

Has a habit of ganging up on you, in the nicest
possible way.

2 tablespoons raspberries
10 ml (1/4 oz) sugar syrup
ice cubes
45 ml (1½ oz) chocolate malt vodka
30 ml (1 oz) vanilla liqueur
fresh raspberries

Muddle the raspberries with the sugar syrup in a cocktail
shaker. Add a scoop of ice, then the vodka and vanilla
liqueur. Shake vigorously and strain into a chilled tumbler.
Garnish with fresh raspberries.

MUDSLIDE

You've been so good — gone for a salad, passed
on the dessert, but whoops, you've slipped up
big time now.

50 g (1¾ oz) dark chocolate
ice cubes
15 ml (½ oz) Kahlúa
45 ml (1½ oz) Irish Cream
15 ml (½ oz) vodka

Melt the chocolate in a heatproof bowl over simmering
water. Dip the rim of an old-fashioned glass in the melted
chocolate, then half-fill the glass with ice. Add the Kahlúa,
Irish Cream and vodka and stir.

— MAHARAJA —

Musky, dusky and deeply exotic — a princely
offering indeed.

2 cardamon pods
15 ml (1/2 oz) sugar syrup
ice cubes
45 ml (1 1/2 oz) vodka
30 ml (1 oz) dark crème de cacao
mint sprig

Pound the cardamon pods with the sugar syrup in a
cocktail shaker. Add a scoop of ice, then the vodka and
crème de cacao. Shake vigorously and strain into a chilled
martini glass. Garnish with a sprig of mint.

— CHOCOTINI —

A chocolate martini! Are we in heaven yet, girls?

50 g (1¾ oz) chocolate
ice cubes
60 ml (2 oz) vodka
30 ml (1 oz) brown crème de cacao

Melt the chocolate in a heatproof bowl over simmering
water. Dip the rim of a martini glass in the chocolate,
or dot the chocolate around the rim. Chill the glass.
Half-fill a cocktail shaker with ice. Add the vodka and
crème de cacao, shake vigorously and strain into
the chilled martini glass.

—— FULL MOON ——

Claim some sanity from the lunar madness and
there'll be howls of thanks all round.

ice cubes
15 ml (1/2 oz) white rum
15 ml (1/2 oz) Kahlúa
1 teaspoon sugar
pinch of ground cloves
pinch of ground cinnamon
150 ml (5 oz) cold espresso coffee
15 ml (1/2 oz) cream

Three-quarters fill a highball glass with ice. Add the rum,
Kahlúa and sugar and stir well until the sugar has
dissolved. Add the cloves and cinnamon, then top up with
the coffee. Float the cream over the top by carefully
pouring it over the back of a teaspoon.

—BROWN COW—

We all love our creature comforts so when you're
onto a good thing, milk it to the hilt.

ice cubes
30 ml (1 oz) Tia Maria
60 ml (2 oz) milk
ground cinnamon

Half-fill a cocktail shaker with ice. Add the Tia Maria and
milk, shake vigorously and strain into a chilled cocktail
glass. Sprinkle with cinnamon.

JAFFA

A creamy concoction kissed with coffee, whisky,
oranges and chocolate. What's not to love?

ice cubes
15 ml ($1/2$ oz) Kahlúa
15 ml ($1/2$ oz) Scotch whisky
15 ml ($1/2$ oz) Grand Marnier
30 ml (1 oz) orange juice
15 ml ($1/2$ oz) cream
shaved chocolate curls
orange twist

Half-fill a cocktail shaker with ice. Add the Kahlúa, whisky,
Grand Marnier, orange juice and cream. Shake vigorously
and strain into a chilled cocktail glass. Garnish with shaved
chocolate curls and a twist of orange.

SCREAMING ORGASM

Oh honey, if it's got you screaming you just *know* it must be good for you.

ice cubes
15 ml (¹/2 oz) Galliano
15 ml (¹/2 oz) Irish Cream
15 ml (¹/2 oz) Cointreau
15 ml (¹/2 oz) Kahlúa
30 ml (1 oz) cream
strawberry

Half-fill a cocktail shaker with ice. Add the Galliano, Irish Cream, Cointreau, Kahlúa and cream, then shake vigorously. Strain into a chilled martini glass and garnish with a strawberry.

SILK
— STOCKING —

Sheer luxury! Why wear anything else?

ice cubes
15 ml (1/2 oz) butterscotch schnapps
15 ml (1/2 oz) advocaat
30 ml (1 oz) white crème de cacao
30 ml (1 oz) cream
white chocolate shards

Half-fill a cocktail shaker with ice. Add the butterscotch
schnapps, advocaat, crème de cacao and cream. Shake
vigorously and strain into a chilled martini glass. Garnish
with shards of white chocolate.

STINGER

It looks harmless enough, but this enticing creature
comes with a nip in its tail.

ice cubes or crushed ice
45 ml (1½ oz) brandy
15 ml (½ oz) white crème de menthe
maraschino cherry

Place some ice cubes or crushed ice in a small highball
glass. Add the brandy and crème de menthe and stir well.
Garnish with a maraschino cherry.

APPLE
BLOSSOM

A delicate drink that will bring a fresh,
petal-like blush to your cheeks.

ice cubes
30 ml (1 oz) apple schnapps
30 ml (1 oz) vodka
15 ml (1/2 oz) white crème de cacao
15 ml (1/2 oz) cream
freshly grated nutmeg

Half-fill a cocktail shaker with ice. Add the apple schnapps,
vodka, crème de cacao and cream, then shake vigorously.
Strain into a chilled cocktail glass and sprinkle with
grated nutmeg.

—GRASSHOPPER—

Crack out the fondue set — the '70s are
back and this joint is hopping.

ice cubes
15 ml (1/2 oz) green crème de menthe
15 ml (1/2 oz) white crème de cacao
60 ml (2 oz) cream
grated chocolate

Half-fill a cocktail shaker with ice. Add the crème
de menthe, crème de cacao and cream. Shake vigorously
and strain into a chilled martini glass. Garnish with
grated chocolate.

TURKISH
MARTINI

Raise a toast to the Ottoman empire
and dream of glories lost.

ice cubes
45 ml (1½ oz) vanilla vodka
30 ml (1 oz) white crème de cacao
10 ml (¼ oz) rosewater
small cube of Turkish delight

Add a scoop of ice to a cocktail shaker, then the vodka,
crème de cacao and rosewater. Shake vigorously and strain
into a chilled martini glass. Garnish with a cube
of Turkish delight.

─── HONEYCOMB ───

Break into one of these before buzzing off to bed and
it'll bee sweet dreams all the way.

ice cubes
45 ml (1½ oz) honey vodka
45 ml (1½ oz) vanilla vodka
15 ml (½ oz) sugar syrup
2 vanilla beans

Add a scoop of ice to a cocktail shaker, then the two vodkas
and the sugar syrup. Shake vigorously and strain into a
chilled martini glass. Garnish with two vanilla beans.

BARTENDER'S TIP
Honey vodka is commercially available but can be hard
to obtain. If you can't find it, use extra vanilla vodka, which
is more commonly available, or infuse your own
(see recipe on page 17).

— HOT TODDY —

A powerful home remedy for dirty rotten head colds.
A cup before retiring and you won't feel a thing.

1 tablespoon soft brown sugar
4 slices of lemon
4 cinnamon sticks
12 whole cloves
125 ml (4 oz/1/2 cup) Scotch whisky

Put all the ingredients in a heatproof jug with 1 litre
(35 oz/4 cups) boiling water. Stir, leave for a few minutes,
then strain. Serve in heatproof glasses.

SERVES 4.

BUTTERED
RUM

Ahoy there! Here's a rummy old trick to beat off the ills and chills of deepest, darkest winter.

1 tablespoon sugar
250 ml (9 oz/1 cup) rum
softened unsalted butter

Place the sugar, rum and 500 ml (17 oz/2 cups) boiling water in a heatproof jug. Stir to dissolve the sugar, then divide among four mugs. Stir 1–2 teaspoons of butter into each mug and enjoy hot.

SERVES 4.

— PORTO FLIP —

Use the very best red port you can lay your hands
on for this curiously complex drink.

ice cubes
30 ml (1 oz) brandy
45 ml (1¹/₂ oz) red port
egg yolk
freshly grated nutmeg

Half-fill a cocktail shaker with ice. Add the brandy, port and
egg yolk, then shake vigorously. Strain into a cocktail glass
and sprinkle with nutmeg.

VIRGINAL

Sometimes it's perfectly acceptable to fake it — for instance, when you have a headache from having had a little too much the evening before. Sitting soft has never been such an appealing option with this memorable collection of marvellous mocktails. So there's really no reason why non-drinkers can't come to the party and have a smashing good time!

JUST LIKE THE REAL THING

IN THESE ENLIGHTENED TIMES we all know one must never drink
and drive, so when a designated driver turns up on your
doorstep with a gaggle of misfits intent on serious mischief, as a
dutiful host it is incumbent on you to ensure our civic-minded
friend isn't left entirely high and dry or at least empty handed!
Of course, it isn't only drivers who need subtle diversions from
inebriating pursuits. There are amongst our population certain
abstemious types as well as those unruly, undisciplined souls
who turn up at a party nursing rather dastardly hangovers and
yet who can't quite manage to stay away! Thankfully, there are
far more interesting creations than just boring soft drink to offer,
or a tired old glass of tap water in which sits a sad squelch of
lemon. Some of the spectacularly innocent mocktails gathered
herein look just like the real thing, without the sting, so your
non-drinking guests will arise with sparkling clear heads the
next morning — unlike you, poor thing. Some you'll want to
drink just for the sheer taste of them. What follows is a fine
sprinkling of bubbly brews and luscious slushes, effervescent
spiders and fizzes, caffeinated creations for a quick kickstart, and
creamy delights you could really enjoy any time of day. A great
proportion of these mocktails are also astonishingly rejuvenating
and bursting with nutrients — so don't be too surprised if you
stumble upon a certain hangover remedy or two …

VIRGIN MARY

Surely one of the few true virgins on the party circuit.

lemon wedge
2 teaspoons celery salt
1 teaspoon black pepper
ice cubes
125 ml (4 oz/ 1/2 cup) tomato juice
15 ml (1/2 oz) lemon juice
1 teaspoon Worcestershire sauce
dash of Tabasco sauce
celery stalk

Wipe the lemon wedge around the rim of a large goblet, then dip the rim in the combined celery salt and pepper. Half-fill a cocktail shaker with ice. Add the tomato juice, lemon juice, Worcestershire and Tabasco sauce and shake well. Strain into the frosted goblet and garnish with a celery stalk.

PIÑA
COOLADA

Enjoy by the pool, or in the pool, any time of day.

125 ml (4 oz/$^1\!/_2$ cup) coconut milk
125 ml (4 oz/$^1\!/_2$ cup) pineapple juice
5 large ice cubes

Place all the ingredients in a heavy-duty blender and blend
until smooth. Pour into a tall glass.

—CINDERELLA—

Cinderella scrubbed the floor and slept in the
hearth but won a waistline to die for — oh, and
a handsome prince.

45 ml (1½ oz) orange juice
45 ml (1½ oz) pineapple juice
15 ml (½ oz) lemon juice
ice cubes

Pour the orange juice, pineapple juice and lemon juice
into a cocktail shaker. Add a scoop of ice, shake vigorously,
then strain into a chilled martini glass.

MIXED BERRY
— AND PINEAPPLE —
FRAPPÉ

Party time for temperate tastebuds.

200 g (7 oz) fresh or frozen mixed berries
225 g (8 oz/1⅓ cups) chopped pineapple
250 ml (9 oz/1 cup) pineapple juice
½ teaspoon rosewater
6–8 ice cubes, crushed

Place the berries, pineapple, pineapple juice, rosewater
and ice in a blender and blend until smooth. Pour into two
tall chilled glasses.

SERVES 2.

FEISTY
REDHEAD

First impressions are deceiving,
she's sweeter than she looks.

12 raspberries
half a small lime, chopped
$1^{1/2}$ teaspoons pomegranate syrup
$^{1/2}$ teaspoon caster (superfine) sugar
160 ml ($5^{1/4}$ oz) ginger beer

Muddle the raspberries and lime with the pomegranate
syrup and sugar in a wide-mouthed medium glass until
pulpy. Top up with the ginger beer.

SPICE ISLAND
TEA

Guaranteed to keep you cool, calm and collected.

1 teabag (such as English breakfast)
large pinch of ground cinnamon
small pinch of ground allspice
ice cubes
15 ml (1/2 oz) lemon juice
125 ml (4 oz/1/2 cup) ginger ale
lemon slice

Place the teabag and spices in a mug and pour in 250 ml
(9 oz/1 cup) boiling water. Allow to cool, then refrigerate
until well chilled. Pour the spiced tea into a large, tall glass
over ice, then add the lemon juice and ginger ale. Garnish
with a slice of lemon.

— GRAPE BASH —

A drink of the vine that won't thrash the head.

10 seedless black grapes
half a small lime, chopped
125 ml (4 oz/½ cup) sparkling grape juice

Muddle the grapes and lime in a tall glass until pulpy,
then top up with the grape juice.

— SWEET TANG —

Give tired tastebuds the razzle dazzle treatment.

150 g (5½ oz/1 cup) fresh strawberries or raspberries
125 ml (4 oz/½ cup) cranberry juice

Place the berries and cranberry juice in a blender and
blend until smooth. Pour into a medium glass.

BARTENDER'S TIP
If fresh berries aren't in season, use frozen instead.

PASSION
BREW

Brew up a batch and wait for the sparks to fly.

125 ml (4 oz/$\frac{1}{2}$ cup) guava juice
pulp of 1 small passionfruit
3 mint leaves, very finely chopped
3 large ice cubes
80 ml (2$\frac{1}{2}$ oz) sparkling grapefruit drink

Place the guava juice, passionfruit pulp, mint and ice in a
cocktail shaker. Shake vigorously, pour into a medium glass
and top up with the sparkling grapefruit drink.

— LEMONADE —

A citrus sling with a ring of sweetness.

egg white
caster (superfine) sugar
juice of 1 lemon
juice of 1 lime
soda water
sugar syrup

Dip the rim of two medium glasses in a saucer of egg white, then a saucer of sugar, shaking off any excess. Chill the glasses. Mix the lemon juice and lime juice together in a jug. Pour into the sugar-frosted glasses, then top up with soda water. Stir in sugar syrup to taste.

SMOOCH

Makes you feel all warm and gooey.

1 large scoop good-quality chocolate ice cream
2 teaspoons hazelnut syrup
15 ml (1/2 oz) good-quality chocolate syrup
2 teaspoons malted milk powder
125 ml (4 oz/1/2 cup) milk
3 Maltesers or chocolate-coated malt candies, crushed

Place the ice cream, hazelnut syrup, chocolate syrup, malt powder and milk in a blender and blend until smooth. Pour into a medium glass and garnish with crushed Maltesers.

ESPRESS YOURSELF

Don't hold back, make a song and dance about it!

125 ml (4 oz/½ cup) espresso coffee, chilled
1 teaspoon honey
a few drops pure vanilla extract
pinch of ground cinnamon
80 ml (2½ oz) cream
3 large ice cubes
extra honey, for drizzling

Place the espresso, honey, vanilla extract, cinnamon, cream and ice cubes in a heavy-duty blender and blend until smooth. Pour into a medium glass and drizzle with a little extra honey.

— TROPPOCOCO —

A tropical daydream that won't send you loco.

half a small mango, peeled and chopped
160 ml (5 1/4 oz) pink grapefruit juice
60 ml (2 oz) coconut milk
2 teaspoons caster (superfine) sugar
3 large ice cubes

Place the mango, grapefruit juice, coconut milk, sugar and ice in a heavy-duty blender and blend until smooth. Pour into a medium glass.

MICKEY MOUSE

An entertaining, all-American classic.

ice cubes
cola
1 scoop vanilla ice cream
whipped cream
3 maraschino cherries

Place some ice in a tall glass. Add enough cola to
two-thirds fill the glass, then float a scoop of ice cream
on top, then some whipped cream. Garnish with
maraschino cherries.

CHERRY
COLA

A bittersweet reminder of all those happy days.

ice cubes
125 ml (4 oz/1/2 cup) vanilla-flavoured cola
125 ml (4 oz/1/2 cup) sour cherry juice
maraschino cherry, with stem

Place some ice cubes in a tall glass. Combine the cola
and cherry juice and pour into the glass.
Garnish with a maraschino cherry.

BLUSHING
── PEACH ──

A beautiful drink that does wonders for the
complexion.

125 ml (4 oz/½ cup) peach juice
125 ml (4 oz/½ cup) almond milk
good dash of Angostura bitters
ice cubes
drizzle of grenadine

Combine the peach juice, almond milk and bitters in a
cocktail shaker with five large cubes of ice. Shake well,
then strain into a medium glass. Drizzle with a little
grenadine and use the tip of a knife to gently swirl the
grenadine into a pretty pattern.

GLOSSARY

ADVOCAAT creamy brandy-based Dutch liqueur made with egg yolks, sugar and vanilla.

AMARETTO a sweet almond-flavoured liquer originating in Italy, made from apricot and/or almond pits with added spices.

ANGOSTURA BITTERS an aromatic infusion of herbs and spices, now made in Trinidad but originally devised as a medicinal tonic by an army doctor in Angostura, Venezuala.

APERITIF a drink taken before a meal under the pretext of stimulating the appetite.

APEROL dark orange Italian aperitif with sweet taste distilled from herbs and roots such as gentian, rhubarb and bitter orange.

BÉNÉDICTINE brandy-based French liqueur spiced with dozens of herbs, invented in 1510 by a Benedictine monk.

BOURBON a corn-mash whisky originating in Bourbon County, Kentucky.

BRANDY fiery amber spirit distilled from grapes and aged in oak, which takes its name from the Dutch word for 'burnt wine'. It can be flavoured with other fruits such as cherry, plum and peach.

CACHAÇA ('ka-shah-sah') clear Brazilian spirit distilled from unrefined sugarcane juice, with a burnt sugar taste.

CALVADOS an apple brandy produced only in the region of Normandy in France.

CAMPARI pungent, ruby-red Italian bitters laced with herbs and quinine.

CHARTREUSE French liqueur flavoured with over 130 herbs and spices, originally created by Carthusian monks as a medicinal elixir. The green version is more pungent than the yellow.

COGNAC fine brandy made from a grape variety grown only around the French province of Cognac.

COINTREAU clear, French, brandy-based liqueur laced with the peel of sweet and bitter Spanish and Caribbean oranges.

CRÈME DE CACAO liqueur tasting of vanilla and roasted cocoa beans, available in white (clear) or brown.

CRÈME DE MENTHE sweet liqueur flavoured with mint and spearmint, available in two varieties: white (clear) or bright green.

CURAÇAO orange-flavoured, spirit-based liqueur available in many colours. It is named after the Caribbean island where the dried bitter orange peel traditionally used in its manufacture was sourced.

DIGESTIF any drink taken after dinner, be it mixed or creamy. Digestifs are reputed to aid the digestion.

DRAMBUIE liqueur blended from fine aged Scotch whiskies, herbs and spices.

FRANGELICO toasted hazelnut liqueur produced in the Piedmont region of northern Italy.

GIN also known as 'mother's ruin' and 'Dutch courage', this clear spirit made from grain and flavoured with juniper berries and other botanicals was developed by a Dutch doctor in 1650.

GALLIANO sweet, yellow Italian liqueur flavoured with herbs, flowers and spices, with a distinct anise flavour.

GRAND MARNIER a luscious Cognac flavoured with the peel of bitter Haitian oranges and spices such as vanilla.

GRENADINE non-alcoholic bright red cordial, used to add colour and sweetness to cocktails.

KAHLÚA dark Mexican liqueur with a toasted coffee flavour.

LIME JUICE CORDIAL thick syrup made from concentrated lime juice and sugar.

LIMONCELLO sweet Italian aperitif flavoured with huge, juicy lemons grown around Sorrento and the Amalfi coast.

MALIBU a rum made in Barbados with coconut extract. Oddly it is bottled in Scotland!

MANDARINE NAPOLEON fine Belgian Cognac-based liqueur infused with essential oils of Sicilian tangerines and herbs.

PARFAIT AMOUR lilac-coloured French liqueur flavoured with herbs and citrus.

PERNOD clear French aniseed-flavoured spirit.

PIMM'S a British institution, Pimm's No. 1 is the commercial version of a gin sling, sweetened with spices, fruits and herbs. Pimm's No. 2 is brandy-based.

PISCO a viscous grape brandy made in Chile and Peru.

POIRE WILLIAM luscious French brandy distilled from the Bartlett pear.

RUM synonymous with sailors, rebellions, pirates and the tropics, this popular spirit is distilled from sugarcane juice or molasses and can be clear, brown or almost black.

SAKE Japanese rice wine.

SAMBUCA anise-flavoured Italian liqueur infused with the witch elder bush and white elder blossoms. The clear version is more widely used, but a stronger-tasting black version is also available.

SCHNAPPS generic term for a spirit distilled from grain or potato, often flavoured with fruits or herbs. The infusion can be dry, like vodka, or very sweet and liqueur-like (such as peach and butterscotch schnapps).

SUGAR SYRUP boiling sugar and water produces a syrup that's easier to mix into drinks than crystallized sugar. Buy it ready-made or make it yourself (see recipe on page 17).

TIA MARIA dark liqueur made from Jamaican Blue Mountain coffee beans.

TEQUILA named after a small town in Mexico, this fiery spirit takes its flavour from the heart of the blue agave, a succulent member of the lily family. It is produced only in three states in Mexico. Gold tequila is aged in wooden barrels for several months, imparting a subtle amber hue.

VERMOUTH a fortified white-wine aperitif flavoured with aromatic roots, herbs, spices and fruit peels, derived from the German word for 'wormwood'. Dry vermouth is pale, and also known as French vermouth. Sweet vermouth may be white (bianco) or red (rosso) and is also referred to as Italian vermouth.

VODKA Russian for 'dear little water', this versatile spirit looks and tastes almost like water. A huge range of infused vodkas are now available (see our recipes on page 17). Smooth operators keep theirs in the freezer.

WHISKY, whiskey Celtic for 'water of life'! Scottish malt whisky is made from spring water and malted barley smoked over a peat fire, matured in oak barrels. Irish whiskey also uses malted barley, but without the smoking process. Canadian whisky, which is often called rye whisky, is made from rye and other grains such as corn, wheat and barley.

DRINK FINDER

ISBN 978-1-7419-6284-0

Concept: James Mills-Hicks
Cover design and layout: Peta Nugent
Production: Kita George

Chief Executive: Juliet Rogers
Publisher: Kay Scarlett

Printed in China in 2009. Reprinted in 2009.

Published by: Murdoch Books Pty Limited, Pier 8/9, 23 Hickson Road, Millers Point
NSW 2000, Phone: + 61 (0) 2 8220 2000, Fax: + 61 (0) 2 8220 2558

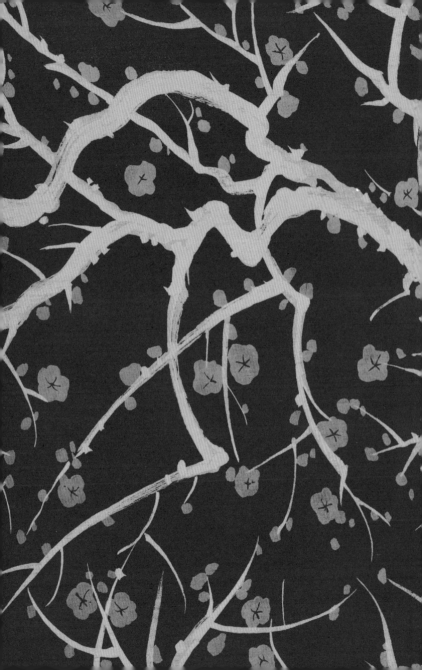